But I Know I Love You

By Steve and Camre Curto

with W. Koenig-Bricker

Dedication

To Camre, who is the strongest, bravest person I've ever known. *(Steve)*

To Steve, who has never left my side. *(Camre)*

To Gavin, our wonderful son … Mommy and Daddy love you.

To all nurses in neonatal intensive care units, who are simply the best.

To all caregivers, who have to shoulder so much responsibility every day.

We'd like to thank …

God for wrapping his arms around our family and protecting us.

Camre's parents, John and Cheryl Carr, for being there when we needed them the most.

Steve's mom, Julie Sullivan, for always lending an ear and Steve's dad, Duane Curto, for his support.

Jessica Smith, Camre's occupational therapist from Galaxy Brain and Therapy Center, for all she has done to help Camre get her life back.

And the University of Michigan Medical School doctors and nurses for getting us answers.

Contents

Preface

The first thing I noticed was that unmistakable hospital smell. I think I've gotten used to it over the years, but maybe you never really get used to that mixture of antiseptic, medication, and fear. At least not once it's been a part of your life. That day, though, the smell was still relatively new, foreign—and a little unnerving.

I nodded at the woman behind the front desk, crossed the lobby, and headed toward the elevator. The door opened and I stepped inside. I drew a sharp breath as the doors glided shut in front of me. I was grateful that I was the only one in the elevator. I didn't want to make small talk about the weather. I didn't want to have to explain why I was here. I didn't want to listen to someone else tell me why they were here. I knew I had to be ready mentally for whatever lay ahead. There was no energy to spare on strangers.

I punched the elevator button. A slight whirr. A jerk. The door opened onto the fourth floor. An alarm beeping somewhere in the distance broke the otherwise heavy stillness. I walked past the med station where nurses and doctors consulted charts and talked in hushed tones. I continued down the hallway and stopped in front of Camre's room. I shut my eyes for a second, then straightened my shoulders and put my game face on as I pushed the door open.

The room was windowless and still, except for the slight swoosh of a blood pressure pump and the flicker of a monitor. I stood at the end of the bed. Camre looked so fragile under the glare of the overhead light. An IV was connected to one arm, and a blood pressure cuff was on the other. Her too-pale face was rounder than usual from all the medications she had been given, and her eyes were shut. She was asleep, but her breathing was so slow and shallow that I had to look carefully to make sure she was still alive. I nodded at her mother, who was sitting in a chair by her side and then came closer and leaned over the rails of the bed.

6

"Hey, honey, I'm here," I said softly as I touched her hand. She opened her eyes and looked up. I knew she saw me, but the emptiness in her eyes told me she had no idea who I was. She didn't know that I was her fiancé. She didn't know that we had a child. I'm not sure she was even aware she was in a hospital. She looked around the room and a flicker of fear appeared, only to be replaced by a blank and empty gaze.

"I'm here," I said again. She glanced at me, closed her eyes, and I turned to her mom. Her mom shook her head and I got the answer I had dreaded—there was no change in Camre's condition. She was still heavily sedated, barely responsive to anything or anyone.

Her mom had been spending as much time as she could with Camre during the day since I was still working full-time and couldn't be there as much as I would have liked. I wanted someone with Camre when the doctors came in, someone who could ask the questions that didn't seem to have any answers, someone Camre knew just in case she suddenly woke up. I couldn't bear the thought of her being alone, but I didn't have any more sick leave or vacation time, so I needed to work. I would visit as often as I could. At least in the mornings and again in the evenings, but during the day, too, if I could get away.

I tried not to let my disappointment show. I knew that Camre's mom was having a hard time seeing her daughter so close to death. Even though her grandson Gavin John was in a neonatal unit in another nearby hospital, this was *her* baby lying in the hospital bed.

"Anyone come in?"

"Only the nurses," she said. "They told me that a neurosurgeon would be coming by soon." We both knew that "soon" could mean anytime in the next twenty-four hours. In the days since Camre had been transferred to the intensive care unit at the University of Michigan medical school hospital, we had learned that doctors make their rounds at odd and unpredictable times. We never knew when they might appear.

7

I turned back to Camre and brushed a strand of dark-brown hair from her forehead. "How are you doing?" I asked. I wanted to sound as normal and as calm as I could, even though I didn't expect a response. She blinked her eyes open and for a moment I thought I saw a spark of the old Camre, but it faded as quickly as it had come. I decided that I must have imagined it as I stared into her eyes, void, empty of any recognition, any personality. I kissed her on the cheek. She turned her face away and I felt a sick feeling wash over me. Camre, the love of my life, the mother of my son, was somewhere beyond my reach.

The afternoon was heavy with the odd timelessness that characterizes most hospitals. Nurses and aides dropped in, checked IVs, took vitals, and sometimes asked if Camre's mom and I wanted something to drink. Occasionally we took them up on their offer. The rest of the time we sat watching the TV with the sound muted so that we didn't disturb Camre, or playing on our phones, or just watching Camre for some sign of change.

An hour or so passed and her mom suggested that I go see Gavin, but I wanted to wait, on the chance that the neurosurgeon came by before dinner.

"You can go," I said.

"No, I'll wait with you."

Just then the hospital door opened and the neurosurgeon who had been called in as the specialist on Camre's case entered. She greeted us with a half-smile and a brief introduction before reading the notes in Camre's chart and listening to Camre's breathing with her stethoscope. Camre stared into the distance, unresponsive. The doctor made a few notes, then turned to face Camre's mom and me. Her face was impassive and professional.

"I'm sorry," she began.

I felt my stomach drop and my knees get wobbly. It is never a good sign when a doctor begins with an apology. I reached out for Camre's hand and squeezed it tight. I hoped she might

8

squeeze it back, but she didn't. We had been waiting for days for precise answers about had happened during Gavin's birth and now the time for answers had arrived. I was afraid of what the doctor would say, but more afraid not to know.

The neurosurgeon's voice was soft and low as she explained that Camre had suffered a severe brain injury while giving birth to our son. I nodded. We had been told that much before. Just looking at her, you could tell that something had happened to her brain. The doctor added that her memory was effected. Again, I nodded. Then the doctor begin to talk about a stroke and brain bleed and short-term and long-term memory loss, using a slew of medical terms. The words started to blur into an almost meaningless jumble. If you ask me what a DW1625 car window is, I'll know what you are talking about, but *medial temporal lobes, hippocampus, neocortex,* and *intracerebral hemorrhage* were just words—words that clearly didn't convey good news.

"I don't understand," I said. Instinctively I reached out again for Camre's hand. She let me hold it, but again it lay limply in my palm. "What are you talking about?" I asked.

The neurosurgeon paused. In the years that have passed since that horrendous day, I now realize that medical professionals find it easier to use formal medical terms when they have to deliver bad news. It's easier on them. It lets them stay more detached. It protects them from the pain that is a necessary part of their job.

"What does this all mean?" I asked again.

The neurosurgeon glanced down, then looked directly at me. "There's no easy way to say this." The words tumbled out. "Camre has total and permanent memory loss, both long-term and short-term. She can't remember anything that happened to her in the past and she can't remember anything that happens to her now. She has no memory at all—of anything."

I heard her mother sob and I felt a sudden tightness in my chest. "Are you sure she can't remember anything? She will never be able to remember anything?" her mother asked. Not her family? Not Steve? Not her baby?"

The doctor shook her head. "As far as we can tell, she has no memory beyond the present moment. The brain injury has wiped out all of Camre's memories, as well as her ability to make new memories. She has no clue who she is or who any of you are and maybe never will."

At that moment, I understood the emptiness I had seen in Camre's eyes these last weeks, the lack of emotion, the inability to recognize me. I was a stranger—a perpetual stranger. I'm sure I must have looked as devastated as I felt. The doctor sucked in a quick breath and resumed her professional stance. "However, this is a very unusual case," she said. "Very unusual. Neither I nor any of my colleagues have ever encountered anything quite like this before, so we don't know for sure what her ultimate prognosis will be. Normally when someone suffers the kind of sustained loss of oxygen Camre did, they are in a vegetative state … or worse. For her to be able to do anything is remarkable."

"Will she ever be normal again?" I allowed myself a tiny bit of hope.

The doctor shook her head. "That's very doubtful." The tone of her voice made it clear that she didn't think it was a possibility. She added, "Her brain is like a computer hard drive that has had all the files erased. The computer can still function, but nothing that was stored on the hard drive can ever be recovered. We think that with therapy, Camre will be able to do some things like feed herself and get dressed. It will be sort of like reinstalling programs in a computer. She may be able to reload programs for walking and talking, but none of the documents or photos—her memories— can ever be restored."

I tried to absorb what the doctor was saying. She went on, "Once she recovers from the physical effects of having blood in her brain—and that can happen pretty quickly--she should be able to do many things. She won't have to be in a wheelchair or live in an institution. She will be able to go home, but she will never be able to live on her own." Her voice resumed a professional edge. "For instance, she might be able to feed herself," she said, "but she won't know how to prepare a meal and she probably won't remember that she has eaten after she has had a meal. Eventually she may be able to shower, watch TV, maybe even read and write. All those normal things we do every day. She won't be a vegetable. She'll still be Camre. It's just her memory that is gone. But don't give up hope," she added. "The brain is remarkable. We are just now learning about its ability to heal itself."

"Heal itself?"

"Yes, we used to think that once the cells of the brain were destroyed, they could never recover. But now we know that it's not necessarily true." She shifted back into professional mode as she went on to talk about neuroplasticity, which is the ability of the brain to change and reorganize itself. She explained that while a brain can't regrow missing parts any more than a foot can regrow a missing toe, it can make remarkable adjustments. "We are just now learning that the functions of a brain that are associated with a certain location in the brain can transfer over time to a different location," she said. "The brain can compensate for damage by making new connections within itself. In other words, even a permanently damaged brain can continue to change and perhaps learn."

"So she will recover? But she won't get her memory back? None of her memories?" I had to ask again, to make sure.

"No." the words were harsh and blunt. I drew a sharp breath as the doctor continued. The word was final. "What we don't know is if she will ever be able to form and hold new memories as her brain heals. We just have to wait and see. The one bit of good news is that we are certain that other areas of her brain outside of memory haven't been affected."

"What does that mean?"

Right now she isn't able to remember anything. It's hard to explain," she added. "But Camre is in a perpetual present moment. All she knows is what is happening right this second … and the next second … and the next. I don't want to give you false hope," she continued, "but we just can't say for sure what is going to happen with Camre. She is a one-in-a-million case."

I asked the question that had been haunting me since that terrible day. "Will she be able to be a mom? I mean, will she be able to do mom things like read to Gavin and see him go to school?" The thought that Camre would never know she was a mom, that she never could be the mom she had wanted to be, was almost unbearable.

The neurosurgeon smiled, the first genuine smile I had seen. "The important thing to remember is that her capacity to love hasn't been lost. We love with the heart, not the mind. Camre might not remember having had a baby, but she can love him. And you."

All of a sudden a new thought made me feel frantic. "What about our baby?" I asked. "What about our son?" Ever since Gavin John Curto had been born a month early by C-section he had been in a neonatal intensive care unit. I had assumed he was there because he was so premature. Now I was worried that whatever had happened to Camre had somehow harmed him.

"As far as I know Gavin is fine," the doctor said. "According to the reports I've read, he's a perfectly normal baby. You'll have to consult with the neonatal specialists, but I'm guessing he will stay in the hospital for a couple more weeks since he was so tiny when he was born, but there is no reason to think that he won't grow up to be a healthy child." She started to leave and then turned back. "You and Camre have a long road ahead of you. You'll be spending a lot of time in doctors' offices," she said. "But you also have a beautiful new baby boy."

After the doctor left the room, I let go of Camre's hand. She seemed to be sleeping, but it was hard to tell because she was so unresponsive. "I'll be back in a little while," I told her mother. "I'm going to go see Gavin."

As I drove across town to the hospital where my son was, everything I had just heard from the neurosurgeon rattled in my head. At first, no one had seemed to know exactly what had happened, but now that we had the results of the medical findings, the answers morphed into more questions. We like to think that doctors have all the answers, but they don't, especially not in cases like this. All anyone could tell me were the medical details of the event; they couldn't tell me what was going to happen because they didn't know. No one knew.

I pulled into the hospital parking lot and took a deep breath. Camre might be in her own world, but there was a new life waiting for me here. At the entrance to the neonatal unit, I scrubbed up as usual and walked over to Gavin's incubator. He looked so tiny lying there with an oxygen tube in his nose, an IV in his arm, and heart monitors on his chest. But his little fingers and toes were perfect and I saw his mother in his face. I have a picture of us from that time— Gavin is sound asleep, his head turned toward the camera. I'm giving a "thumbs up," and I have a half-smile on my lips. As I look at the picture today, I can see the pride in my eyes and the joy I felt knowing that I was now a father, something I had thought about my entire life. But more than that, I see my determination.

I leaned over the crib and promised my boy that I would never let him down. I was his dad and I was here for him for the rest of my life. But more than that I made a promise to myself. I vowed right then and there that I would stay strong, no matter what. We were a family—Camre, Gavin, and me. Absolutely nothing was going to change that.

"I love you and your mom, I whispered. " And I always will."

Back to the Beginning

My whole life I've really liked being around kids. One of my earliest memories is imagining what it would be like to have a family. For whatever reason, I've always had a lot of patience with kids. I guess it was because I somehow knew that I was born to be a husband and a father. Even as a kid myself, I would wonder what it would be like to be a dad. I thought about how I would teach a kid the things I knew, how I would to listen to him (or her), how we would celebrate the milestones of growing up. Heck, I even thought about what it would be like to be a grandfather! I just knew that one day I was going to have a family of my own. I also knew that when the time came to make that commitment, I would make it with everything in my being.

The other thing I've always known about myself is that I'm good at fixing things. If it's broken, I consider it a personal challenge to figure out how to repair it. My family comes from a long line of car lovers, so tinkering with cars was built into my life, but fixing "stuff" was always part of who I was. So it wasn't a big stretch when, after a year of college, I took a job as a Safelite AutoGlass repair technician. Yes, I was one of those guys you see in the commercials going out and fixing broken car and truck windows. I really liked my job. I was proud to be among the top technicians in my district, and I took pride in my ability to fix any broken windshield quickly and easily.

Once my love of fixing things and of kids intersected on the job. I was working near a school when a teacher brought her class out to watch. She asked if I minded and, to be honest, I was kind of flattered. I gave an impromptu lesson on how to install car windows. The kids watched with fascination as I took out the cracked windshield and replaced it with a new one. I could tell most of them had no idea that car windows were removable. When I was done, the teacher commented that I had been really good with the kids. I thanked her and went on to the next job. Now that I think back, I realize she was hinting that I might want to ask her out. But although I always wanted to be a husband and a father and I knew I was good with kids, I also knew this wasn't the right time. Even into my late 20s, I was content to be "Uncle Steve" to my nieces and nephews and the children of some of my friends. I always figured that when the time came, I'd be ready. But I waited so long some of my family—like my mom—began to wonder if the time would ever come.

The right time came one ordinary afternoon in August of 2009. If you've ever been to Michigan in the late summer, you know that the heat and humidity can be brutal, especially when you have been working outside. When Friday rolled around, I was totally ready to kick back, watch some TV, and relax in the air conditioning. My roommate was gone, so I was looking forward to some alone time with my favorite college football teams. I drove home, changed clothes, and settled in on the couch.

I was trying to decide if there were some leftovers in the refrigerator or if I should order in a pizza when my phone rang. I'm sure there was a brief moment when I thought about ignoring it, but I picked up.

"Hey, Steve. What are you doing tonight?" my buddy asked.

"Not much. Just hanging out. Why?"

"Some of us are getting together for dinner at Legends. Want to come?" I hesitated, and he added, "Come on. You need to get out."

"Nah," I said. "I'm really beat. I think I'm just going to stay home. Next time, okay?"

I could hear the disappointment in his voice as he said, "Well, if you change your mind, we'll be at Legends like I said."

I hung up the phone and began flipping through the TV channels looking for a football game to watch. None of the matchups really caught my attention and the thought that maybe I should meet up with my buddies crossed my mind for a second, but I dismissed it. I was debating what toppings to put on the pizza when all of a sudden it felt like someone was shouting in my mind, "Steve! Get off that couch. Put on some decent clothes and get to the restaurant."

Now I'm a pretty practical guy, so this seemed like nonsense. I ignored it and continuing debating between pepperoni and sausage. But the thought wouldn't go away. In fact, it got louder. This time I swear I heard it say, "Steve, get off that couch. Put on some decent clothes and get to the restaurant."

Again I dismissed it, but it kept coming back. In fact, it got more insistent—"GET OFF THAT COUCH!"

I figured I was just tired or overheated and was imaging things, but the thought never let up. Finally, I couldn't stand it any longer. I gave up. I flipped off the TV and headed to the shower. All the time I was getting cleaned up, I kept thinking that this was just crazy, that I should just stay home like I had planned. Every time I hesitated, the thought returned: "GO TO LEGENDS!"

Nothing like this had ever happened to me before … and to be honest, I'm thankful it's never happened again.

For whatever reason, I put on dressier clothes than I would usually wear to an impromptu gathering, hopped in my truck, and drove to Legends. Now Legends is a popular local sports bar known for its beer, wings, and big-screen TVs. All the way there, I kept thinking that this was just the craziest thing I'd ever done, but I decided to make the best of it. After all, I'd been thinking about ordering a pizza and Legends was also famous for its great pizza. I decided I'd get a bite and a beer and then head back home to my couch,

My friends were all gathered at a table in the back behind the pool tables and they waved me over. I knew most of the people who were there that day, but sitting near one end of a long table was this gorgeous girl I'd never met. Her dark brown hair fell in curls over her shoulders and her green eyes flashed with a combination of mischief and strength that hit me like the proverbial ton of bricks. I said a general "Hi, guys" to the table and then focused on the girl.

"Hello," I said, trying not to sound too awkward. "I'm Steve."

"I'm Camre. Nice to meet you," she said, holding out her hand. I recognized her name because we had a lot of mutual friends who had mentioned her now and then, but we had never been in the same place at the same time. Looking back, it's funny that we had never met before, but now I realize it just wasn't the right time before that night.

We shook hands and I sat down in a vacant seat two chairs over from her. At first, I talked with the guy between us, but I kept looking over at Camre. Finally, I leaned over him and asked her a few standard questions, like where she worked. I barely remember her answers because I was immediately lost in her smile. As we waited for our meals, we talked about the usual stuff ... the weather, football, the crazy people I met on my job.

We just kept leaning across the guy between us, talking about anything and everything until he finally gave up and, with a knowing grin, moved over a seat so we could be together. I immediately hopped into his vacant chair without missing a sentence.

"So do you have a pet?" I asked.

"A Newfoundland," she said.

"Oh, what kind of dog is that?"

"Big, black dog," she said. "I've always had a Newfoundland. My grandmother started the Newfoundland Club of San Diego and my family has bred them for forty years."

"Oh, wow," I said.

"They are the sweetest dogs."

"I don't know that I've ever seen a Newfoundland."

"We call them Newfies," she said. "They're really good with kids."

17

"Cool," I said. *How good are they with boyfriends?* I wondered.

When I look back, I'm amazed at how quickly we hit it off. We kept talking and again, it sounds like a cliché, but time stopped. I don't even remember what I ate, but I'm pretty sure it wasn't pizza. Camre probably had something with chicken—chicken is still one of her favorite foods. We were just chit-chatting back and forth without stopping. Apparently, it became obvious that we were really into each other, because none of our friends even tried to join us. By the end of the meal, it felt like just a few minutes had passed. That's how absorbed I was in our conversation. Later, I asked Camre about that first meeting and she agreed that something special had happened, something that we both felt, but couldn't quite put into words. Somehow we both knew that this was a pivotal moment in our lives.

When dinner was over, I wasn't ready to let her go home, so I asked her if she was going to go to the bonfire one of our friends was having at his house. Having a bonfire is a favorite summer and fall activity in the part of Michigan where we live, so going to a fire would be a natural continuation of the evening. I think I held my breath until she said she would meet me at our friend's house. I've never asked her what she was thinking at the time, but I know that I was thinking that if she had said she wasn't going, I wouldn't have known what to do. I just didn't want to stop talking with her. I like to think she felt the same way.

We drove our separate cars to Lake Fenton, one of several lakes in our area. It's a popular recreation area where people come to water ski, swim, sail, and fish. We pulled up in front of a three-story glass-fronted house sitting on a hundred feet of lakefront at the end of the road. In my job, I got to see a lot of houses, but this one was especially nice. Even though I grew up in the suburbs of Detroit, I had always loved the outdoors and I remember thinking that one day I'd like to have a house on a lake. At the time, I wondered if Camre would like to live on a lake.

We parked our vehicles and walked together to the firepit at the edge of the lake. Sometimes people think that it's easy for a guy to make small talk, but trust me, when you are falling in love, your tongue has a mind of its own. I think I said something stupid, like "Nice night for a fire," but fortunately, I can't quite remember what else I might have said. What I can remember is the heavy feel of the summer air on my face and the smell of burning leaves and damp wood. I remember the sound of gently lapping water from the shore combined with the crackle of the fire and the murmur of voices. And I remember Camre's smile.

People were milling about, watching the sparks from the fire fly into the darkening sky. Camre and I pulled up a couple of chairs and sat down close enough to feel the heat and keep the mosquitoes away. I wanted to be sure we were close enough so that the light would let me see every feature of her face.

We began to talk. And talk. And talk. Time slid away as we talked about everything imaginable. As the night wore on and the fire started to burn down into glowing embers, the voices around us began to die away. It was after midnight when I realized most of our friends had already called it a night, but I was still focused on Camre. I didn't want to be too pushy, but I wanted to know everything about her ... not just things like where she worked, but about her dreams and hopes.

Finally, as the last embers were glowing, I said, "I guess we'd better get going," We walked back to our cars under a star-studded sky and I remember thinking I wanted to kiss her, but I also didn't want to be too pushy. Finally, I leaned over, kissed her on the cheek, and asked her for her number. I'll admit my heart was racing a bit and I probably was holding my breath as I waited for her response. She smiled that smile that even today makes my heart skip and gave her number to me. As she drove off and I climbed into the cab of my truck, I rested my hands on the steering wheel and took a deep breath. I knew right then that she was the reason I had to get off my couch and go to the restaurant that day. I knew she was the one I had been waiting for.

Green-eyed Girl

I could barely sleep that night. My thoughts were filled with images of a dark-haired, green-eyed woman. I'll admit this was new for me. Although I had always thought I would be a dad and a husband someday, as I said, I wasn't in any hurry. In fact, I think my mom had just about given up hope on me. But, as I said, there was—and still is—something special about Camre.

The next morning I drove to my first appointment. All the while I was installing the windshield, I was thinking about Camre's number in my phone. I must have started to call her at least a dozen times, but shoved the phone back in my pocket each time. That night after work, I looked at her number and almost pushed the call button but stopped myself. I thought about texting her, but that didn't seem quite right either. I wanted to hear her voice, not just read a text from her.

I'm sort of embarrassed to say that I went back and forth about calling or even texting for three days! As I look back, I think I waited at least one day too long to get in touch. Although Camre can't remember, I know her well enough to realize that she had probably already written me off as one of *those* guys. In my defense, I didn't want to seem too pushy or too eager, but the real reason was that I was afraid she was going to turn me down. Now getting turned down isn't the end of the world most of the time, but I knew that Camre was different and if she didn't want to see me again, I didn't know what I was going to do. I even thought about showing up at her place of work, but then decided that would make me seem like a stalker. So I just kept putting off making the call.

Finally I worked up the courage to call. Sometimes girls think it's easy for guys to make the first move, but trust me, when you really like someone, it's not that easy at all. As her phone rang, I realized I was holding my breath. *What if she didn't answer? What kind of a message could I leave? Should I even leave a message? Should I call back?* After what seemed like an awfully long time, she picked up.

"Hi."

"Hi there. This is Steve, remember me? We met at Legends and went to a bonfire." The words tumbled out awkwardly.

"Yes, I remember." Her voice sounded a little cool and I kicked myself for waiting so long to call.

"Hey, I really enjoyed talking with you and I wondered if you'd like to have dinner with me sometime?"

She paused. I don't think I started to breath until she said, "Yeah, I'd like that. What did you have in mind?"

I suggested that I pick her up the next night about seven. "Is there someplace you'd like to go?"

I heard a little bit of a laugh in her voice as she said, "No, you choose. Surprise me!"

Looking back, that was just classic Camre. Always up for an adventure, always ready to try something new. It's that spirit, that inner confidence that first drew me to her and still amazes me today. It's that determination to grasp life with both hands that has enabled us to get where we are today. It's the reason that Camre has defied all the odds.

To say that the next day passed both all too quickly and way too slowly is an understatement. When I finished my last job, I raced home to shower and get ready. I knew that this wasn't going to be just any old first date, so I wanted to make the best impression possible. I probably spent more time getting ready that I ever had for any date … except maybe prom in high school. I decided on khaki slacks, a blue-grey colored shirt, brown dress shoes … and my watch. I always wear a watch, even in this age of cell phones.

Once I was dressed I thought about what else I could do to show that I was really interested without being too forward. I decided that going old school by bringing a bouquet of flowers would be a good idea. I wasn't exactly sure what to get; roses seemed a little too much and a houseplant seemed sort of silly, so I choose a large mixed bouquet with orange, yellow, red, and blue flowers that I spotted at the local flower shop. They were bright and cheerful and, as sappy as it sounds, they sort of reminded me of Camre. The florist wrapped them in green paper, and I laid them carefully on the passenger seat as I drove to her house.

Camre lived with her cousin on a circular development not too far from my place. As I turned onto the road, I realized that my heart was pounding a little faster than usual. *It's okay, Steve*, I told myself. *Everything is going to be okay. You've got this.* I pulled up in the driveway and looked in the rearview mirror. I shaved my head at the time, so I knew that my hair was going to be okay, at least. I made sure that my collar was straight and reminded myself that this was what I had been waiting for since the bonfire. I picked up the flowers, making sure that they hadn't left a mess by dripping water on the seat and hopped out of my Cherokee.

I walked up to the front door, put the flowers behind my back, rang the bell, and waited. She must have been close by because it opened almost immediately. She was wearing a dress—she had worn jeans the day we met—and she looked even more beautiful than I remembered. I don't know exactly what I said, which is probably a good thing. I know I handed her the flowers and was both relieved and pleased when her face lit up with the most amazing smile.

No matter what has happened over these past years, she still has that amazing smile to this day. I remember one time, during one of the seemingly endless doctor appointments that followed her brain injury, she was sitting on a hospital chair with electrodes all over her head when I snapped a picture. I can recognize the pain and fear in her eyes, but despite it all, she is giving me a thumbs-up and that always-radiant smile. That's Camre through and through. No matter what happens, she finds the best in it.

She took the flowers and put them in a vase. All of a sudden, a big—120 pounds big—fluffy, black bear of a dog ambled up and slobbered all over my pants. I had tried so hard to make a good impression and now I was covered in dog slobber. It was the first time, but it certainly wasn't the last. I think I'm destined to live the rest of my life with big, slobbery dogs that eat everything in sight. Camre laughed as I went to the kitchen and wiped off the drool as best I could before escorting her to my truck.

Our first date was at Redwood Steakhouse and Brewery in Flint, Michigan. From the outside, it looks like an old-fashioned lodge and inside it reminds me of a really fancy cabin out in the woods. It definitely has a "Michigan" feel to it. I picked it because I wanted to take her to a nice place (with good food), but I didn't want it to be over-the-top either. Remember what I said about it not being all that easy for guys? Well, deciding where to go on a first date can be one of the challenging moments. Especially when the girl has said she wanted to be surprised. On the drive over there, we picked up our conversation just where we had left off at the bonfire. Once or twice, I kicked myself for having waited so long to call, but then I'd glance over at Camre and I knew that things were happening just the way they should.

Redwoods turned out to be the perfect place for a first, real date. In fact, it's still one of our favorite restaurants. As I look back, the thing I remember the most is thinking how lucky I felt to have paid attention to the voice that kicked me off the couch. I was raised in the Lutheran Church and have always believed in God, but I am convinced that the voice I heard that night came directly from heaven. It's the one and only time I've heard anything like it, but it was unmistakably directed toward me. And it wasn't going to take "no" for an answer.

I ordered a steak and asparagus, and Camre ordered chicken. It's funny how details like that stick in your mind, but even though I still like steak and Camre still likes chicken, every memory of our first date is gone for her. No matter how many times I remind her, no matter how many times we talk about it, Camre doesn't remember a single thing about that night. She knows we went on a date, but she can't remember it.

It's difficult to explain what it's like because her brain injury is so rare. She knows that things have happened, but she can't remember them. For instance, she knows she worked as a service rep, but she can't remember anything about the job. What she does know and can "remember" are emotions she has felt. Everything else is lost to her devastating brain injury. So she "knows" we had a first date and she "knows" we had a good time because she can "feel" it. Now, when we go to Redwoods and I tell her that this was where we went on our first date, she smiles and nods her head. She doesn't remember anything from that night, but, as she tells me, she knows she is glad she went!

But back to that evening. The night went all too fast and when I took her home, I was already planning our next date. We stood on the porch, I kissed her, and that was it. I knew she was the one for me. Fortunately, Camre was as ready for the relationship as I was. We made plans to meet the next day … and the next … and the next.

From that day on, we were together as much as possible. I would come to her place after work, and we would hang out together on the weekends. At the time, I was living with a buddy, but I had already decided I wanted to look for a place of my own. Camre was ready to have her own place as well, so I began looking for a house to buy. About eight months after we met, I found a place on a lake that I really liked. Fortunately, Camre was as excited to live on a lake as I was, so when I was ready to move into the house, it just seemed natural that she and her dog would move in too. It was never a question that Camre and her Newfoundland were a package deal. Camre and I both loved being in the middle of all the trees and wildlife, but her dog was in heaven with all the new smells and places to explore.

Like most couples, we had some adjusting to do once we actually were living together all the time. After we had been together for a few months, we had an argument. Now it wasn't a huge argument, but it was big enough that we decided we needed to put the brakes on our relationship for a little while. We decided we both needed to think about what we wanted, so Camre went back to her parents' house and I stayed in the lake house. It wasn't like we were furious with each other; it was more like everything had moved so quickly from our first meeting that we both felt like we needed to step back and make sure that this was what we really wanted.

It didn't take more than a day for me to realize that the separation wasn't what I wanted. I would come home to that empty house and think about Camre. I'd get up in the morning and think about Camre. I knew then that all I wanted was to be with Camre and build a family with her and I would do anything and everything to make that a reality.

We stayed apart for about a week. Then we both admitted that we needed to be together. Camre came back to the house and we've been together ever since. It's not that we've never had another argument. We disagree like every couple, but the decision we made to be there for each other has never wavered. Even though we didn't formalize our relationship with marriage for a few more years, we had made a commitment to each other right then and there. This was for the rest of our lives, no matter what.

It was that commitment that has helped us get through the darkest of days and it's that commitment that keeps me going now. Even when Camre doesn't remember how or when we made a commitment, she knows we have a commitment, and she knows that neither of us will ever let it go.

Baby on Board

Once we were together for good, Camre and I settled into a routine. She continued at her job as a service rep for a phone company and I continued to replace windshields for Safelite. We were a pretty typical couple, I think. We were involved with our friends and families, and while we always knew that we wanted to have a family of our own, we weren't in a great hurry. We were content to be a couple and to build our relationship. Looking back, I'm glad that we had that time together. As I said, Camre can't remember events but she does relate to emotions and she "knows" that we were very much in love. And we were.

A couple of years into our relationship, we decided to take a winter vacation to Florida. Winters in Michigan can be brutal. By February we were both needing some warm sunshine. We splurged to stay at a resort hotel right on the beach in Clearwater. Although it wasn't our honeymoon—we didn't get married for a couple more years—it was the perfect honeymoon location. Blue sky, turquoise water, white-sand beach. I'm not exaggerating when I say it was a picture perfect spot. At first, we had a room with a partial view of the ocean, but when the plumbing backed up, we got upgraded to a full ocean view with a balcony. For the next couple of days, we hung out in blue cabana chairs, alternating between the beach and the pool. We ate great food. Enjoyed the sunshine. Walked the beach and collected sea shells. It was one of the most special times in our relationship, and it is one of the greatest sadnesses of our life that Camre doesn't remember anything about it.

Once Camre suffered the brain injury, it was like someone took an eraser to her entire memory. She doesn't remember anything about growing up. Her childhood, her teen years, everything before the brain injury is completely gone. Now, years later, she has some partial memory of things that happened after the injury, as long as she has been told it over and over. That's why she finally knows my name and Gavin's name. One thing she seems to remember is numbers. For

27

instance, later in our relationship, we took a family vacation to Hawaii. If I ask her about our time there, she can tell me what room we stayed in—17G—but she doesn't remember anything about the place or what we did. It's one of those odd things about the brain. Rote memories, things that Camre has been told over and over, go into a different location that wasn't affected by the injury. In addition, some things, like numbers, are stored in a different place as well. But regular memories, like what she ate for dinner last night, still don't encode.

This brain glitch is one of the most frustrating things for both of us. Sometimes, when she doesn't think I'm watching, I catch her looking so sad it makes my heart break. I try to just tell her that it doesn't matter that she can't remember. What matters is that we are a family and that we love each other, but I know that it bothers her. As she slowly regains some ability to create new memories, the realization that some things are lost forever becomes even more difficult for her. But I've always said she is the strongest person I know … and she is. Once we came across a sign that read, "Those who cannot remember the past are condemned to repeat it." I have a picture of Camre in a bright-pink striped top pointing up to the sign and smiling that amazing smile. Camre knows she doesn't know and remembers she can't remember, but yet she smiles.

When we were on vacation in Florida, what we had always talked about happening, happened—we got pregnant. Of course, we didn't know that we were going to become parents right then, but when we looked back, we realized it couldn't have been more perfect. We were in a fantastic place, we were deeply in love, and we both absolutely wanted to have a child.

Camre knew that she was pregnant before she told me, because she started feeling queasy and nauseated in the morning. Like a lot of guys, I was pretty oblivious to it all, because we hadn't actually been trying to have a baby. We took a chance one night on vacation and … well, the rest is history. There's an old saying, "Man proposes, but God disposes." That's true for us. We hadn't planned to have a baby right then, but God—and Gavin—had different ideas. Maybe that's too much information. Camre tells me that sometimes I share too much, but that's just me! Anyway, when we came back from vacation, little did we know that we had begun the most dramatic roller-coaster ride of our lives.

The day I found out we were going to be parents started out like any other day. Camre had suspected something, but she hadn't mentioned anything to me. She had a day off. She called me at work and said she had something to share with me when I got home. I was sort of "yeah, okay" about it all. I should have known that something was up, but I just figured she was going to tell me that she got a new coffee maker or something. When I got home, she pointed to the counter. One of those pregnancy test-strips was lying there with a pink band showing.

I picked it up and looked at it. "What does that mean?" I asked, like the proverbial idiot. She gave me one of "those" looks. "We're going to have a baby?" Her radiant smile told me all I needed to know. After I hugged her and we twirled around the kitchen in a happy daze, I stopped and asked what I now realize was a foreshadowing question. "How are you feeling?" I was reassured when she said that other than morning sickness, she was feeling fine. The odd thing is that she really did feel fine during the first two trimesters of her pregnancy.

Camre shared the news with her mom, and then I called my mom. "Hey, are you sitting down?"

"Yes," she sounded wary.

"Camre and I are going to have a baby!"

"You're kidding!?"

"Nope, you are going to be a grandma again."

"That's wonderful!" The joy in her voice made me excited all over again.

Me, a dad! It was something I'd always wanted, but now it was really happening.

Camre and I both wanted to know the sex of the baby as soon as we could, but we had to wait a couple of months until Camre was far enough along for an ultrasound. As we waited those weeks, I thought about what it would be like to be a dad to a little girl who was a mini-me to her mom. I imagined reading to her and watching princess movies with her. Then I thought about being a dad to a little boy who looked like me and who would share my love of sports and the outdoors. Finally, I realized that I could read and watch movies with a son and share sports and the outdoors with a daughter. I suddenly didn't care what we had as long as the baby was healthy.

It was a June day when we went for THE ultrasound appointment. I didn't think I was going to be anxious, but I was more nervous than I expected as the technician rubbed the wand over Camre's belly. The image that appeared on the screen just looked like swirls and blobs, but it all meant something to the technician, because she asked if we wanted to know the sex. I peered at the screen, but I couldn't see anything that indicated either a boy or a girl.

Camre and I said that we wanted to know, but not right away, so the technician wrote something on a piece of paper, slipped it and the ultrasound image into an envelope and handed it to us with a broad smile. I carried that envelope like it was made of gold as we left the clinic and crossed the parking lot to our truck. When we got in, we looked at the envelope and then we looked at each other.

"Do you want to wait and have one of those gender-reveal parties?" I asked. Camre shook her head. "No, I want it to be a private time with just the two of us."

"Shall we look now?"

We both stared at the envelope and I handed it to Camre. She opened it and pulled out the paper the technician had inserted with the sonogram image. Broad, scrawling letters announced "It's a Boy!!" with a smiley face beneath.

I yelled, "A boy. It's a boy!" I thought my heart would burst out of my chest. I had never been happier in my life. Now the fact that we were pregnant was undeniable. I had seen a picture of our child. Our baby. Our son. Nothing prepared me for the rush of feelings that overtook me. Camre was crying, and I started crying, too. I was going to be a dad! Actually, I was a dad! I just hadn't met my son yet.

When we called our families, they were delighted for us. I think my mom secretly would have liked us to have a little girl, since she already had four grandsons, but she has never let on. She just said how exciting it was that our son would have a whole pack of cousins to grow up with. Camre's family, on the other hand, had only daughters, so a grandson was an unexpected delight. I'm not sure that her dad actually believed that the baby was going to be a boy until he was born! It is one of the great blessings of our lives that our son is growing up in the midst of such loving and supportive grandparents, aunts, uncles, and cousins.

Gavin was due in November. Because we knew the months would go by fast, we got busy putting together a nursery and preparing all those things that expectant parents do. Now, at the time, even though Camre and I were fully committed to each other for life, we hadn't made our relationship formal with an engagement. I think one of the reasons I was reluctant was because my parents had divorced when I was a teen and I knew that I never wanted to get a divorce. Once I got married, I wanted it to be for life. I realize that isn't exactly the best reason not to become engaged to the mother of my son, but it's the reality. Some of my own fears meant I was a little slow in getting around to asking Camre to marry me. To her credit, she never pushed me, but shortly after we found out that we were going to have a baby, I decided to "put a ring on it." Deep down, I knew that we were in it for the long haul, but I also knew that I didn't want to become a parent without a formal commitment and neither did Camre. One day, without telling Camre, I went ring shopping. I

31

knew what kind of jewelry she liked, but I also wanted it to be a surprise. I finally settled on a single

solitaire diamond with smaller diamonds on each side and a matching wedding band.

I had asked her father for her hand in marriage sometime earlier, so he knew that the

proposal was coming, but I kept the ring hidden for a couple of months. I guess I was just waiting

for the "right time." Actually, I wanted the engagement to be memorable, which is ironic since

Camre can't remember any of it. I finally decided that the Fourth of July would be ideal. Each year

there is a huge fireworks show over the lake where we lived. I thought that proposing by fireworks

would be very cool. We owned a pontoon boat, so I decorated it with handmade signs that said

"Love Boat." That evening, I told Camre that I wanted to watch the fireworks from the water.

When she saw the Love Boat signs, she made some remark, but I just passed them off as a fun idea I

had. We floated out to the middle of the lake, where we could look back at our house with its dock

and fire pit—I've been partial to fire pits ever since that first night Camre and I met, so I made sure

our house had a big one by the lakeshore—and across to the houses on the other side.

I have a picture I took when we were out in the water, waiting for the show to begin. Camre

is wearing a blue and white top and her baby bump is just starting to show. Her hair is blowing in

the breeze and she has a huge smile on her face. But even though we didn't know there was

anything wrong at the time, there's something in her eyes that hints at the trouble to come. She

looks a little distant, a little drawn, but at the time the pregnancy was going great, so we weren't

worried.

The first fireworks lit up the sky. I pointed to them to get Camre to turn and face away from

me. Once she did, I pulled out the ring box, got down and one knee and said, "Hey, Cam, look over

here." She turned around and her mouth opened in complete surprise. "Will you marry me?" I asked

and held out the ring. She nodded, whispered yes, and began crying. I slipped the ring on her finger

just as another round of fireworks went off. She tells me that I have a romantic streak, and I guess I do, but proposing on a Michigan lake in the middle of fireworks seemed pretty darn perfect to me. We let our family and friends know and for the next few weeks, neither of us could have been happier.

I know that somehow I was meant to go to that restaurant and meet Camre, but shortly after we got engaged, something else happened that still gives me chills. Before it will make sense, I have to back up a little. I grew up in the Lutheran church. Almost literally grew up in the church because my grandparents lived across the street from it and my grandfather helped build the church building. My parents were married there and we went to services every Sunday and Wednesday. As I got older, I drifted away. I never gave up my faith, but it just wasn't all that important to me. It's hard for me to admit it, but I was more concerned about friends and work than I was about going to church. God just wasn't all the important to me at the time. I figured I could handle life on my own and didn't really feel the need to ask God for help, but with a baby on the way, I had been doing some soul-searching and evaluating my whole life. Getting engaged made it even more imperative. I wondered if we could handle all the expenses of raising a child and I worried that, despite my desire to be a dad, if I was really going to be a good father and husband.

Then something happened that changed my outlook.

I had just finished a big job at a customer's house. I was writing up some paperwork when a lady comes running out of the house and up to my rig. I immediately thought either there was something wrong or they had a complaint. I rolled down my window, but before I could say a word, she asked, "Do you believe in God?"

I thought it was an odd question and I wondered if she was going to hand me a card with some Scripture verse, but I said, "Yes, absolutely."

She then said, "I want you to know that I get these visions and God speaks to me." I immediately began thinking *Uh oh, now what?* She continued, "I had a vision that you have a fiancée and she's pregnant." Right there my jaw hit the floor. I said, "How do you know that?"

"God showed me a picture in my mind of your family. I just want to let you know that everything is going to work out fine. You are a strong man. You have a beautiful family. Now I know that one of your main concerns is how you are going to support this child. You are wondering how you are going to do all this. You are worried if you are going to be a good father. A lot of things are going through your head right now. Don't worry. You are going to be a great dad. You are going to be able to handle whatever happens. Don't worry. Everything is going to work out. You guys are going to be financially okay. You are going to be great parents. You guys are going to be okay."

I didn't know what to say. I just sat there thinking *I don't even know this lady and she is telling me my future.* Before she walked back into the house she reassured me again that things were going to work out. I stayed in my rig, pretending to complete the paperwork, but I was really just trying to absorb all that had just happened. There I was, just doing my job, and some lady tells me that she had a vision about me and Camre.

The next thing I did was call my mom. She confirmed my feeling that this was really a sign from God. That was the start. That was when I began rebuilding my connection with God. With everything that has happened to us, I often think about what that woman said before we knew anything was wrong, and how she reassured me that everything was going to work out. Knowing this has become my rock. When things got really hard, and they did, I would say to Camre, "Everything is going to be okay." Even now, when she can't remember that I ever told her about the woman with a vision, I say the same thing: "It's all going to work out."

And it always does.

Shower of Concern

It wasn't long before Camre had a tiny little baby bump. Although sometimes she thought she just looked fat, I told her I thought she looked more beautiful than ever. She had a kind of glow about her that I can't describe, and it sounds sort of corny, but every time I saw her, I knew that I had been given divine direction that night when I decided to go out to dinner instead of staying home and watching college football.

Neither of us knew first-hand what to expect from a pregnancy, but Camre felt fine and the ob-gyn assured us that the baby was growing on schedule. We could hardly wait until we felt the first movements, the first kicks, the first signs that there was a little person in there waiting to meet us. We kept up our work routines, and while Camre was getting tired of the morning sickness, everyone assured us that it was normal and it would end soon.

Once she was well into the second trimester, the nausea had pretty much tapered off. She was putting on weight and finally thought she looked pregnant, not out of shape. Not long after our Fourth of July engagement, though, she began to feel a little off. She couldn't explain exactly what she was feeling, but she sensed some kind of change. We figured it was just part of being pregnant in the heat and humidity of the summer. At our next visit, the doctor assured us that everything was on schedule with Camre and the baby. We even have a sonogram from that time that shows Gavin giving us a "thumbs up" from the womb, so we didn't pay any attention to her odd feelings. Looking back at pictures with the gift of hindsight, I can see some little signs that things weren't quite right, like puffiness around her eyes, but the baby was growing right on schedule and other than being tired, Camre seemed fine. Like most people, we assumed that if there were a problem someone in the medical profession would let us know.

By the time the third trimester began, things started to go downhill rapidly. We went out for burgers one evening and Camre got violently sick that night. We thought it must have been food poisoning, but I had eaten the same thing and didn't get sick. Camre never stopped vomiting that night or the next day. We knew that food poisoning can last a couple of days, so we still weren't terribly concerned, but when Camre got sicker and sicker and couldn't keep down anything, not even water, we realized that something more serious was going on. We thought maybe she had the flu, but she didn't have a fever or any other signs, so we made an appointment and went in to see the doctor.

When the doctor weighed Camre, she expressed concern that Camre had lost quite a bit of weight since her last visit, but we all continued to assume that she had some sort of bug. I even joked that maybe it was the return of, not morning sickness, but all-day sickness. The doctor ran some tests, which didn't show anything definite, so she prescribed some anti-nausea medication and told us to come back in a couple of days. When we returned a few days later, Camre was still vomiting and had lost even more weight. On that visit, the doctor told us that our baby wasn't growing at the rate he should have been.

That's when the fear set in. Not only was Camre getting sicker by the day and no one could figure out what was happening, now our baby was having issues. Of course, Camre was unhappy because she was so sick, but her major worry was that her sickness was hurting our baby. I can remember sitting with her, holding her, and telling her that none of this was her fault and that we would get through it. I reminded her of what the lady had said about everything being okay. I'm not always sure I believed what I was saying, but I knew that I had to be strong for all of us—me, Camre and our son.

That was the start of the dark time of our lives. The doctors ran test after test, but they couldn't agree on a diagnosis. All the while, Camre just kept throwing up. The medication the doctors had prescribed helped somewhat. It didn't take the nausea away completely, but it calmed things down, and we began to count the days until our baby would be born. We had already decided on his name—Gavin John. I remember talking to him every night, telling him how excited we were to meet him in a few weeks. That's one of the hardest things for Camre—not remembering how happy and excited we were planning for the birth and how much we were looking forward to seeing our little boy—but the blessing is that she doesn't remember how worried we were, either.

People have asked if Camre had the same thing that Prince William's wife, Kate Middleton, has with her pregnancies. The answer is no. Kate has a condition that causes her to be severely nauseated and sick her entire pregnancy. It's like morning sickness on steroids. Camre had "normal" morning sickness that actually went away like it was supposed to. Getting violently ill in the last trimester was puzzling to the doctors, but they kept telling Camre to keep trying to eat as much as she could so that the baby had as long as possible to develop. The doctors explained that the longer Gavin could stay in the womb, the better it would be for him. When they told us that, we realized that there was a very real possibility that our baby would be premature, but we still didn't completely understand the danger that Camre herself was in.

At this point, Camre took a leave from her job because she was so weak and tired. She began spending the days at her mom's, basically lying on the couch, trying not to throw up. The doctor prescribed Zofran, a strong anti-nausea medication that is administered through a pump. It operates a lot like the insulin pump they give a person who has diabetes. A tiny needle was inserted under the skin of her belly, and she wore a battery pump on a fanny pack on her waist. Basically, the idea was to get a small dose of anti-nausea medication around the clock to keep the level steady, rather than taking a pill every eight hours and waiting for it to wear off. The Zofran did help with the nausea, but it didn't take it away completely. However, Camre said that the pump didn't really hurt, which was a small blessing, and she started to gain a little weight back. We began to feel a bit more encouraged.

Our encouragement took a nose dive in early September. My mom and Camre's mom had put together a shower for our family and friends at an upscale restaurant called the Brick Street Grill in Grand Blanc, Michigan. Both of us were planning on going, but Camre was a lot more excited than I was. I was just sort of going along for the ride. The morning of the shower she woke up feeling awful. "I really want to go," she said with a quaver in her voice. "I really want to go, but I don't think I can."

"Are you sure?" I asked. "I'll be there with you. And your mom will be there."

She shook her head.

"You can decide a little later this afternoon after you see how you are feeling," I added, trying to be encouraging.

She shook her head more emphatically "I just can't," she said, her eyes filling with tears. "I don't feel right. I just don't feel right. I'm just too tired. I can't do it."

I was shocked. Nothing ever got Camre down. No matter what happened, she always managed to push through. For her to say she couldn't make the shower should have been a fire-alarm warning to both of us. She had been having some bad days, but she had been having some pretty good days as well. It was completely out of character for her to admit she didn't feel well enough to go.

"Okay," I said trying not to sound too worried. "You have to do what's best for you. Do you want me to stay home with you?"

"Of course not," she said. "One of us has to be there!" I really didn't want to go, but she insisted. "Who's going to open the gifts?" she asked. "Your mom? My mom? I don't think so!"

I told her I'd take lots of pictures and text her while we opened presents. I remember looking in the mirror just before I left. I was wearing a short-sleeved blue shirt—I figured it was appropriate for a baby boy shower—and I had my glasses on instead of my contacts. I pulled on my favorite Detroit Tigers, Old English-style "D" baseball cap, looked myself in the eye, and said, "You've got this, Steve!" Little did I know how often I would say that over the next years.

At the shower, people asked about Camre. They questioned why she wasn't at her own shower. Since not a lot of people knew what was going on, I had to explain that she wasn't feeling well. As I talked about how sick she had been and the Zofran pump and all, I began to realize just how serious the situation was. I can remember thinking, *Wow, pregnancy is no joke.* That was the moment when it dawned on me that pregnancy was a lot more dangerous than I thought it was and that something really bad could happen to either Camre or Gavin or both of them. Up until then, I had passed off everything as just a part of pregnancy, but the reaction of family and friends opened my eyes to the seriousness of her condition.

I was determined to make the best of the day because all of our family and friends were there and while I was growing increasingly worried, I didn't want to worry everyone else. I tried to downplay the situation while we did the usual shower thing of food and cake. When it came time to open the gifts, I really missed Camre. As I look back, if I had known then what I know today, that day would have given me a little insight on what it was going to be like for the next several years. Camre would be with us, but she really wouldn't be present. I was going to have to do all the mom and the dad things for our son.

Despite the shadow of Camre's illness, the shower actually turned out to be a lot of fun. My mom gave us a crib and dresser set that could later convert into a toddler bedroom set. We got all kinds of boy outfits, like a little baseball uniform, and a blue and white suit. We were also given a handmade blanket from a family member. We even got a sock monkey just like the one I had when I was a kid—the kind that is made from those brown-and-white socks with red heels that become the mouth. I made a few jokes about the monkey and then when my mom gave us a particularly goofy little outfit, I said, "Really, Mom? Really? You think we are going to put him in this?" Even she had to laugh at that.

As the shower wound down, I couldn't wait to share with Camre. I knew I had done my best with the situation we were in, but it wasn't the way we had hoped. When I got home, she was lying on the couch watching TV.

"Hey, honey, how are you?" I asked.

"I'm okay," she said, but I knew she was putting on a brave face so as not to worry me. That's one of the things that has always amazed me about her. I keep saying that she is the strongest, bravest woman I've ever met but it's really true.

"So what did we get?" she demanded.

"Hang on," I laughed. "They're in the truck." I brought in the armloads of gifts and set them on the floor next to her. We went through the things I had opened, and she "oohed" and "aahed" appropriately. I told her about my mother's nerdy outfit and we both laughed. Because I didn't want her to feel left out, I had saved a few gifts for her to open. She unwrapped some outfits and baby toys while I did my best to make it feel like a real celebration. In addition to the presents she unwrapped, I brought along the baby register where the big-ticket items like the crib and a mattress were listed, so we got to go through all of that together and plan how we were going to fix up the nursery.

Even though it was a happy time, with each gift, Camre got more teary-eyed until she was finally just bawling. "I don't understand," she sobbed. "I don't know why I'm sick. I don't know what I'm doing wrong." I reassured her it wasn't her fault and that she wasn't doing anything wrong, but she just shook her head and said, "I'm so frustrated. I'm not getting any better and nobody seems to know what's happening." There wasn't anything I could say. I felt the same way. I had always believed that doctors could figure out what was wrong and at least offer some solutions, but with Camre, they seemed just as confused as we were. I sat beside her and held her as she cried. "Everything is going to be okay," I said over and over. Finally, she sat up, wiped her eyes, and opened the last gift. It was this little hat that looked to me like a smiling dog with googly eyes.

"Oh, a dog hat," I said. "I guess they knew you loved dogs."

"I think it's a bear," Camre said, holding it up and pointing to its ears.

"It looks like a dog to me," I said.

"Dogs don't have round ears like that," she said. Then she grinned. "Maybe it's a monkey. It can go along with the sock monkey," she laughed.

"I still think it looks like a bear," I said, "but we can call it a monkey hat."

"Whatever it is, it's really cute," she said, tucking it back into the package. "Gavin is going to look adorable in it."

And he did. The day I brought our little monkey home, I remembered what his mom had said while we were waiting for him to be born and I made sure that he was wearing that "monkey hat."

Downward Turn

The best I can say about the next couple of weeks after the shower is that Camre was more or less stable. She didn't get much better, but she didn't get much worse, either. Since she had to take a leave from her job because of her sickness, we developed a temporary new normal. I'd bring her to her mom's house in the morning when I went to work. She'd spend the day with her mom, taking it easy and resting. After work, I'd pick her up, we'd go home, have dinner and she would head to bed. She didn't have much energy for anything else. What she was trying to do more than anything was keep eating so that Gavin could continue to grow.

The Zofran pump was a necessary hassle. With its help, she threw up only every couple of days instead of several times a day. Some women actually change their own pumps, but because the doctor wanted to monitor Camre for dehydration, she would go in regularly to the office. A lot of the time she would be given IV fluids while she was there because she got dehydrated easily. Having those IVs wasn't pleasant, but it saved us trips to the ER. Despite the inconvenience, Camre was willing to do everything she could to make sure our baby was safe. As things finally settled down, Camre was doing well enough that the doctor ordered a home nurse to come to our house to administer the IVs and the change the Zofran pump. She wasn't really gaining much weight, but she wasn't losing much either, so her ob-gyn kept encouraging her to hang in there while Gavin was developing. Gavin was growing; not quite as much as he should have, but he was growing steadily. Each visit to the doctor we would anxiously wait for a report and were relieved when his heart continued to be strong, and he continued to kick and move.

Camre always felt a little better after getting IV fluids, but one time something went wrong. Instead of the IV fluid going into the vein like it was supposed to, it ended up infiltrating her arm. Her arm swelled and became hard and painful, so we had to make a trip to the ER. There isn't much that can be done when an IV slips out of place except to wait and let the excess fluid be reabsorbed.

Looking back, it was just another sign that things weren't heading in the right direction, but at the time it just seemed like one more relatively minor frustration.

The day that everything fell apart started like most other days. Camre went to her mom's and I went to work. I had been feeling sort of anxious ever since the shower, but I can't say that I was feeling more anxious than usual that day. I was just sort of "normal" anxious. A lot of the reason I was pretty calm was because Camre was very calm. Even when she was really concerned, she didn't dwell on it. I gave her a kiss and told her I'd see her after work.

I was assigned to a mobile Safelite unit, so rather than working in a shop, I drove around my territory fixing windows on-site. When I had free time between clients, I'd give Camre a call. She always assured me that she was doing okay. "Don't worry. Everything is going to be okay," she said, echoing my own words.

That afternoon when I picked her up, she mentioned casually that her throat felt funny. When she talked, her voice sounded a little raspy. I asked her if she thought she should go to the ER, but she declined. "I'm fine," she said. "Maybe I'm catching a cold."

"Okay, but if you start feeling bad, let me know."

A little later she calmly came up to me and said, "Steve, I think something's wrong. I think maybe we should go to the ER. I seem to be having trouble catching my breath."

I tried not to panic as I walked with her to the car. She was calm and collected, but I could tell her breathing was getting more strained. By the time we got to the hospital, she was having a lot of trouble talking.

"Can you breathe?" I asked.

"Yeah," she said, "but it's getting harder." When we explained to the desk what was happening, we were immediately assigned to a room. A nurse came in and took Camre's vital signs.

She was hooked up to some oxygen and we began the long wait that everyone who has ever been in the ER understands all too well.

We waited … and waited … and waited. Nurses came in occasionally and an ER doctor popped his head in the door once. We had a lot of questions, but nobody was around to give us answers, so we just hunkered down to wait. Once she got some oxygen, Camre began breathing more easily, but she really wasn't able to talk at all, so she began writing notes instead. I called her mom and explained the situation. Her mom lived only a few minutes from the hospital, so she said she would come immediately if we needed her. At the time, we said things were okay, so we just kept waiting to see what was going to happen.

By the time a couple of hours had passed, I could tell that Camre was getting worried, but typically she really was more concerned about the baby than she was about herself. Because no one had panicked when we first checked in, we still thought that whatever was happening wasn't all that serious. At one point, a new nurse came in and took Camre's vital signs. She frowned a little and I wondered what she was thinking. "This looks to me like pre-eclampsia," she said, quickly adding, "but I'm just a nurse, not a doctor, so I can't make that diagnosis."

I had never heard of pre-eclampsia. If I had, I would have made several different decisions over the next few hours, but at the time I naively asked, "What's that?" The nurse explained that pre-eclampsia was a problem that can occur late in some pregnancies that increases the risk for both mother and baby. She reassured us that if it were pre-eclampsia, there were medications that could be given that would help, so we didn't really give it much more thought. As I've said, at the time we trusted that the medical personnel would know what was going on even if we didn't. In retrospect, I wish I had asked more questions about pre-eclampsia because, as we later learned to our shock and sorrow, pre-eclampsia can become eclampsia very quickly. In fact, untreated eclampsia is one of the leading causes of death of both mothers and babies throughout the world. When it isn't caught in time, it creates a lot of problems for the mom, like high blood pressure, kidney and liver issues, swelling, and shortness of breath. If it isn't treated immediately, seizures can begin. At that point, pre-eclampsia becomes eclampsia. When that happens, the baby has to be taken by emergency C-section to save its and the mother's life. It's one of the risks of pregnancy that no one really talks about.

The nurse took more vitals and left the room. No one other than that one nurse ever mentioned pre-eclampsia again, so we didn't give it any more thought. However, if I had to do it over, I would have insisted that a doctor take a look at Camre to determine if she was pre-eclamptic. I would have paid closer attention to all of her vitals and demanded that someone figure out if her breathing problem was from her throat or her lungs. But hindsight is 20-20 and I did the best I could at the time. With everything that happened later, I still have to remind myself that I did my best. If I didn't, I'd be eaten alive by guilt.

After about four hours in the ER, someone decided that since Camre was 33 weeks pregnant, they probably should keep her overnight just to be sure that nothing more severe than the loss of her voice was going on. She got into a wheelchair and was transported to a regular medical room at about 10 p.m. We called her mom and said that she was going to stay the night, so her mom came over to sit with us for awhile. Now I wonder why she wasn't taken to labor and delivery, but at the time, everyone thought she had at least another month before Gavin would be born. Again, if I had to do it over, I would have insisted that she be taken to labor and delivery immediately.

Being in a hospital is like being a stranger in a foreign country. You are surrounded by both odd silence and strange noises. People pass outside your door in a hurry, yet you wait and wait for someone to come into your room. You doze, but you never sleep. You are always on alert and yet you don't know what to expect when someone does come in. You hope to see a doctor, but doctors come at random moments. As you wait, time itself begins to lose meaning. All you do is wait.

45

About midnight, Camre's mom encouraged me to go home and get some rest. "You've got to go to work in the morning," she said. "Go home. They say that Camre is fine and I'll stay here with her."

"Are you sure?" I asked.

"Yes, I'm sure. If anything changes, I'll call you right away."

I didn't want to leave and said I'd stay, but Camre scribbled a note, "I'm just fine. Go home!"

"But I'm worried about you," I argued.

She shook her head and mouthed the words, "Go home. I'm fine."

Camre is a very strong, very stubborn woman and because no one was indicating that the situation was critical, I reluctantly agreed. "Be sure to call me if anything changes," I said to her mom. Camre rolled her eyes and shoed me out of the room.

A couple of times on the way to the parking lot I almost turned back, but I had to be at work early in the morning and I knew Camre's mom would let me know if I needed to come back. However, as I think about it, leaving Camre that night is one of the greatest regrets of my life. Obviously, nothing can change the fact I wasn't with her. I can't get a mulligan or a do-over on my actions. I have to accept that I did what I thought was right at the time, but I've wondered so many times about how things might have been different if I had stayed. Deep down I know that my presence probably would not have changed anything, but that hasn't stopped me from asking *What if? What if I'd asked more questions about pre-eclampsia? What if I had insisted that a doctor find out what was going on? What if I had only stayed?* I realize that I can't change the past and so I try not to dwell on it anymore. It sometimes helps that I know Camre doesn't remember that I wasn't there, and even if she did remember, she wouldn't blame me.

But I remember.

I didn't sleep much that night and was feeling pretty tired when I texted Camre first thing in the morning. She still couldn't talk, but she texted back that she was feeling a little better. She added that her mother had gone home and she was just lying in bed, watching TV, and waiting for the doctor to come in. "No worries!" she wrote. She added she thought she would be released in the early afternoon, so I planned to get off work early and pick her up. I wondered for a minute why they would release her if her throat was still bothering her, but as I've said before, we didn't really question medical decisions at the time.

As I began to replace the first broken windshield on my job list, I'm sure the client thought that I wasn't very friendly, but I was becoming more and more anxious. I just wanted to get the job done and get back to the hospital. Now I almost hate to admit it, but while I was worried about Camre, I was worried about a lot of other things as well. I knew that the woman who had the vision had told me things were going to be okay, but I didn't completely believe her. I mean, who would believe someone who just came up to you out of nowhere and said that God had a message for you. On one level, I did believe, but on another level, I was still worried. I worried how we were going to get all the things a new baby would need, since we had counted on Camre's income and she had to quit work early. I worried about how I was going to juggle being a new dad with the demands of my job. I worried about mortgage payments and car payments and a lot of other things. Looking back, I realize that I was worried about a whole lot of material things that ultimately weren't nearly as important as I thought they were. But I was still worried.

Over the course of the morning, Camre and I texted a few more times. She said she was still feeling pretty good and she thought that she would go home in the afternoon. I vividly remember her last text: *Everything's good. I'm fine. The baby is fine. I love you.*

It was the last thing I heard from her before her brain injury.

Unexpected Arrival

Camre's last text reassured me, but I still wanted to finish up work as soon as possible so I could get back to the hospital. I felt guilty about leaving her, even though she had wanted me to go, even insisted that I go. About an hour after our last text, I was vacuuming up some glass on a job site when I felt the work phone in my hip holster ring. My first thought was that I was going to have to go on another job, but when I looked at the number, my heart sank. It was my mom. She never calls me on my work phone, so I instantly knew that something had to be very wrong.

"Steven, Steven, Steven. Camre had the baby!"

"What? She had the baby? Is everything okay?"

"I don't know. The hospital called and said they had tried to reach you, but you didn't answer your phone." I knew instantly what had happened. I had left my personal cell in my rig, so between that and the vacuum, I hadn't heard the call. Time literally stopped. I was in complete shock. I told my mom I would be there right away and she added that she was on her way as well.

I left all my tools, all the paperwork, everything right there at the job site. I slammed the side door of the van shut, hopped into the driver's seat, and spun my tires as I peeled out. I did have the presence of mind to call my boss, tell him that Camre had the baby, and give him the address where I'd left the equipment, but after that nothing mattered except Camre and our baby.

It was about a five-minute drive to the hospital, but I made it in three minutes. It's a good thing there wasn't a cop on the road. All the while, I kept wondering what had happened, if Camre was okay, if Gavin was okay. I was really disappointed that I hadn't been present when Gavin was born, but most of all I felt guilty that I hadn't been there when Camre needed me. Even now, I get little twinges of guilt about that. I think it's one of the reasons that I am so determined to live up to my responsibilities as a husband and a dad. I never want to let my family down ever again.

I screeched into the hospital parking lot, jumped out of the truck and began running. The only parking spots were way in the back. Grabbed my phone. Sprinted. Outran the hospitality cart. Nope, gotta go. Good half-mile, right? Track had been my sport in high school and now I was running the fastest mile of my life. I shoved through the front door of the hospital, slowed down long enough at the information desk to shout "Labor and delivery?" The receptionist pointed to the right. I ran right, through one set of doors, then another set of doors, took another right and skidded to a halt when I saw Camre's parents standing in the hallway. I rested my hands on my knees as I tried to catch my breath.

"What happened?" I panted. "Where's Camre? How's the baby?"

Her mom explained that Camre had to have an emergency C-section, but they didn't have any more information about her or Gavin's condition. She said that when the hospital couldn't reach me, they had called her. She didn't have my work phone, so she called my mom, who then called me. Because they lived so close, her parents had come right over to the hospital to wait for my arrival. "Do you know where Camre is?" I asked again. They said they thought she was still in the delivery room, but no one had really given them any information. "What about Gavin?" I asked. Just then a nurse came out of the door on the right, wheeling a tiny bundle on a cart.

She paused and looked at me. "Mr. Curto?"

"Yes." I caught a glimpse of a red face, an upturned nose, and dusting of brown hair wrapped in a white blanket.

"We have your son. We need to get him into intensive care, but you can visit him in a few minutes. There's a waiting room right over there. We'll come get you when he's ready."

My son. My boy. If I could I would have taken that bundle from her right then and there I would have. It seemed completely surreal. My son was in one room, Camre was in another, and I was in a hallway. It was not the way I had ever imagined becoming a dad. Instead of a dream come true, this was more like a nightmare. I've said that I'm a fixer but there was nothing I could do to fix this. All I could do is wait and pray. It was one of the most hopeless feelings of my life.

Camre's parents sat down to wait on a lonely little bench in the hall. I was too nervous to sit for long, so I just paced back and forth in front of the door, waiting for it to open again. After what seemed like forever, but actually was only about ten or fifteen minutes, the nurse came to get me. Our first stop was the scrub station. Everyone who comes into the neonatal intensive care unit (NICU) must wash up thoroughly before visiting a baby. As the warm water ran over my hands, I glanced around. If you've never been in a NICU, it's a very odd place. On one hand, the cries of babies remind you that it's filled with new life. But because all the babies there are either very premature or seriously ill, you also sense fear and worry. During the weeks Gavin spent there, I saw some things that no one should have to see, a lot of very sad things, like crying and shaking babies who born to drug-addicted moms and babies who were not going to live much longer. I saw parents whose hearts were broken, as well as some who, after months, were finally able to take their children home. It's one of the most difficult places a parent can ever be in.

I have to give a huge shout-out to the nurses in the NICU. They deal with worried parents, sick babies, high-tech machines, and constant stress, yet they are among the most caring and compassionate people you ever want to meet. Just being around them always made me feel like Gavin was going to be fine and that whatever happened, I could handle it.

The nurse led me to a table where Gavin was screaming his head off. He was sixteen-and-a-half inches long but he weighed only four pounds. My first thought was *Oh my God, he's Camre, Junior. He looks just like his mother.* My next thought was how tiny he was, lying there on a blue-and-pink striped blanket, with monitors on his chest and an oxygen tube in his nose. I reached out and gently touched his hand. "Hey, buddy. I'm your dad." He squeezed my finger with a shockingly tight grip. My little muscle boy!

"He is little," the nurse said to my unasked question, "but he is healthy. We have him here because he is so little and he needs some time for his lungs to develop. But don't worry. He's a perfectly healthy preemie."

"Oh, thank God." I looked at his ten perfect little toes. I think every parent can understand that what you want the most is to have a healthy child. I was delighted to have a son, but I was more grateful that he was healthy. I rubbed my fingers along his cheek. He was so precious, so beautiful. I know that every parent thinks their baby is beautiful and I was no different. I just wanted to sweep him up in my arms and hold him, keep him safe. The nurse said that I could hold him a little later, as soon as they had finished with all their checks and were certain that he was stable. I touched his little head and thought again was how much he looked like his mom. Instantly, I shifted from pride and joy to panic and worry.

"Camre, his mom? Do you know where she is?"

The nurse said that she probably was still in surgery. She explained that when a woman has an emergency C-section, the first priority is to get the baby out. Then they sew up the mom and make sure that she is stable before taking her to a room. I stayed with Gavin for a few more minutes, until the nurse said they needed to get him into an incubator. I went back out to tell Camre's parents what I knew and let them know they could see Gavin in a little while. We kept waiting for news about Camre and eventually we were told that she was being transferred to the intensive care unit (ICU) on the third floor and we could see her in about an hour. I didn't really understand the significance of going to ICU instead of labor and delivery, but too much had happened in too short of a time for me to ask many questions.

At the time, none of us knew what had happened to Camre other than she had had a C-section. It wouldn't be for a couple of weeks that we learned she had experienced a severe brain injury from loss of oxygen and had completely lost her memory. That first day, we all assumed she just needed extra care because of the rush of the surgery.

Had I known then what we faced, that I was going to be on my own, raising a child and being a caregiver, I would have been a lot more worried. But at the time, I just took things as they came. Actually, that's the way I still handle things. I just take them as they come and remind myself that I can get through it. I've learned that if you face issues as they arise and not spend too much time worrying about the future or regretting the past, you can do almost anything. That's one thing I've tried to remind Camre and teach Gavin: You are always stronger than you think you are and you can do more than you think you can. "I've got this." Sometimes I have to remind myself as well, but I truly do try to live by that motto.

My mom arrived shortly after we learned that Camre had been transferred to ICU. She and Camre's parents were allowed into the NICU to meet their grandson. As I said, my mom was excited, but Camre's parents were really excited because he was the first boy in the family in a very long time. We took a lot of pictures that day because I figured that Camre would want to see what her baby looked like when he was first born. Little did any of us realize that those pictures were going to become the only memories Camre would ever have of Gavin as a newborn. Even now, when we look at them, I know that she doesn't remember anything. I see the sadness in her eyes when for the thousandth time she realizes that she doesn't remember and it breaks my heart.

Finally I was told that I could go see Camre. I left Gavin to the care of the nurses and his doting grandparents. As I rode the elevator to the third floor, I wasn't sure what to expect. All I had been told was that she had continued to have trouble breathing after the surgery so she was intubated and sedated. I steeled myself before entering the unit, which was a good thing. If you've never had to spend time in an ICU, count your blessings. It's like NICU times ten. Like the NICU, it is dark and quiet, but the feeling of hope and new life that comes with babies is completely absent. Everyone in ICU is fighting for their lives. It can feel as if death itself is hiding in every corner.

As I was shown to Camre's bedside, I tried not to look at any of the other patients, but I couldn't help it. Some of them were all alone, but others had one or two people by their beds. Machines beeped. Monitors whirred. Alarms sounded. I don't usually feel afraid of most things, but I felt myself clenching my teeth, so I knew I was more anxious than I realized.

Camre was lying on her back, with a tube down her throat, an IV in her arm. The jagged line on a monitor recorded every beat of her heart. She looked like she was sleeping, but she was so still I peered closely to make sure she was still breathing. When I saw the faint rise and fall of her chest, I let myself relax a bit. She didn't look anything like the spunky, determined woman I had left the night before. Her usually thin face was puffy. Her skin was drawn and colorless.

"Hey, honey, I'm here," I said, touching her hand. I watched for some sign of recognition, some response, but there was nothing.

"What happened?" I asked the nurse on duty. She said that she would get a doctor to explain as soon as she could. That's sort of the way it went over the next several days. I'd ask questions, someone would say that they would try to get an answer, but no answer would come. As I look back, I realize that the doctors themselves didn't know exactly what had happened, so they were trying to put us off until they understood the situation better. I get that's what was happening, but it would have been so much easier on all of us if someone had just given us whatever information they had at the time. Waiting and not knowing anything is so much harder than waiting and knowing something.

I stayed by Camre's side for as long as I could, watching her breath, and looking at her heartbeat on the monitor. She never moved, never stirred. Eventually, the nurse gently suggested that I go get some rest, adding that they would call me on my cell if there were any change.

Reluctantly, I left Camre to tell our parents what little I knew about her condition. As I headed back downstairs to the NICU, I realized the one bright spot was that I was now the dad I had always dreamed of being.

I scrubbed up again and located Gavin's incubator. I wanted to hold him more than anything, even if it was just for a few seconds. The nurse put him in my arms and my mom snapped a picture on her phone. That photo in particular always chokes me up. I'm sitting in a chair holding Gavin for the first time and kissing the top of his head. You can't see my face or Gavin's because I'm bent over, holding him against my chest. I remember thinking at the time how amazing it was to be a dad and promising that I would always be there for him and his mom no matter what.

It's a promise that even today I would give my life to keep.

The Flight of Her Life

The next twenty-four hours all sort of run together. What I remember the most—besides going back and forth between Gavin's and Camre's beds—is being totally confused. I kept trying, without success, to get some answers from someone. It just didn't make any sense that Camre could be fine one minute, then have a C-section and be fighting for her life the next. I kept asking what was going on, but the nurses in ICU couldn't really tell us what had happened because they didn't know themselves. They'd say that they would get a doctor to talk to us, but even when a doctor did show up, we just got the run-around. Now that I look back, no one really knew exactly what had occurred because it was so odd and unusual; they had never experienced anything like it before. Not that understanding would have made it any easier at the time.

After a couple of hours—during which time I made several trips between the NICU to see Gavin and ICU to see Camre—I was finally told that Camre had had a grand mal seizure. The doctor explained that they had to do an immediate C-section to save both her and Gavin's lives. They thought she might have had a stroke because of the seizure, but they really didn't know for sure. All they could tell me was that she was in very serious condition.

I had heard about seizures before but I didn't know what a grand mal seizure was. Without getting too technical, a grand mal seizure is what people think about when they imagine a seizure. The person loses consciousness and begins to twitch uncontrollably. Usually seizures are caused by epilepsy. Looking back, this first seizure should have been a warning for Camre's battle with epilepsy that continues to this day. However, this first one was caused because Camre actually did have pre-eclampsia, as that one nurse had suspected. Because she wasn't diagnosed quickly enough, pre-eclampsia rapidly devolved into eclampsia, putting both Camre and Gavin into an immediate critical state. The doctors were worried that her soaring blood pressure and seizures were cutting off oxygen to the baby, so she was raced to surgery in order to save his life—and hers. It wasn't until several days later that we learned that during the C-section, Camre had suffered a five-to-eight-minute loss of oxygen to her brain. I still don't know exactly what happened during those few hours, but piecing the events together, I think that because her throat was so swollen, it took longer than it should have to intubate her when they were putting her under for the C-section. The resulting lack of oxygen caused a stroke, which caused bleeding in her brain, which caused her catastrophic memory loss.

Sometimes people ask me why they didn't do a tracheotomy when it became apparent she wasn't breathing. I know they almost did one, but I'm told they had decided that it would have just added to her risk of death. At this point, it really doesn't matter. What happened, happened. We can't undo the past.

When we were right in the middle of it all, I had so many emotions it was difficult to remember exactly what I was feeling. I never knew it was possible to be over-the-moon happy and completely devastated at the same time, but that's how I felt. I was so sad seeing Camre in that hospital bed, but I was also excited and happy about Gavin. I was relieved that Camre was still alive, I was worried about what was going to happen to her. I was thrilled to be a dad, but I was anxious about how I could take care of an infant. I bounced from one feeling to the next.

All afternoon, I kept going back and forth between Camre and Gavin. I'd be up on the third floor with Camre, saying to her, "Come on, honey, come on. Pull through. Please, please, I hope you are okay." Then I'd go down to the NICU and talk to Gavin. "Hey, buddy, how you doing? Daddy loves you. Everything is going to be okay. I'm here for you." In between, I'd be praying, "God, help me. Help my family."

My dad, my sister, my brother, my sister-in-law, all came by to see Gavin, as well as some of Camre's relatives, but nobody could be in the ICU but me and Camre's parents. About 10 p.m., everyone else went home, but I needed to be with Camre. I pulled a very uncomfortable chair up to her bedside. The nurses gave me a blanket and I just sat there holding her hand, talking to her. "Hey, you just gave birth to the most beautiful little baby boy in the world. Wait 'til you see him. You are going to be so proud." At one point, I start of started talking to myself as well, just going over everything that had happened. I can remember saying, "Everything is going to be all right" over and over. That's become our family's saying. No matter what happens, we just tell each other, "Everything is going to be all right." You have to believe it and I really do. I really do believe that no matter what happens, it's going to be all right.

All night long, Camre was completely sedated and unconscious. She didn't know that I was there, but it didn't matter. I needed to be there with her in case she woke up. I needed to be there because I still was feeling guilty about not being with her when she had the seizure and when Gavin was born.

After a very long night with thousands of interruptions and very little sleep, morning finally came and the doctors started to make their early rounds. Camre had several doctors on her case. Finally, one of them told me that they were going to decide about removing the tubes in the next couple of hours. Once that happened, they would then be able to evaluate what else might be going on.

The nurses assured me that she was stable enough for me to get some breakfast and visit Gavin. I did both, then returned to the ICU to sit by her side and think about life and how much ours had changed in just a few hours.

I kept waiting to see if they were going to remove the tubes, but eventually I was told that the doctors wanted to wait another day. They wanted to make sure she was going to be able to breath on her own before they took her off the oxygen and lightened up the sedation.

I spent the rest of the day once again going back and forth between Camre and Gavin. Unless you've spent time waiting in a hospital, you don't know how surreal it is. You keep waiting for someone to tell you something. You are exhausted and worried, but you are on high alert at the same time. I think the best way to describe how I was feeling was anxious. I was anxious about Camre. I was anxious about Gavin. I was anxious about my work. I was anxious about what was going to happen. If I could have paced, I would have, but the only thing I could do was sit by Camre's side and hold her hand. I kept thinking about how just a couple of days before everything seemed to be on track for a normal delivery. Now, instead of us becoming a family at home, Camre was fighting for her life and I was facing the very real possibility of having to take care of an infant by myself.

One thing I'll never understand about hospitals is why it takes so long to make a decision, but finally, in the wee hours of the morning, they decided to pull the tubes. Camre's mom was with me and they sent us out of the room while they did the procedure. I'm actually glad I wasn't there because it was hard enough seeing her lying there without having to watch them do whatever they did. They let us back in the room and we began waiting again.

That was a hard time. The sedation gradually wore off and Camre began to drift in and out of consciousness. It became clear that something was seriously wrong when she opened her eyes, but didn't recognize us. I can remember looking at her and thinking, "Camre's not there!" Sometimes she would blink and I'd have this wave of hope that she was getting better. I tried to tell myself that she was coming out of a medicated coma and it was just going to take a little more time, but then she would immediately sink back into a blank stare. It was then I began to realize I could lose Camre. Even if she was still physically with us, the woman I loved, the woman who had been Camre, was somewhere far beyond my reach.

That sinking realization was confirmed when she suddenly began talking—not to me, but to her hand. It was almost like she was talking on her cell. "Yep, yep. You're there? Okay, you wanna go fishing?" The longer this continued, the more worried I became. I asked to see an on-call doctor immediately. When he arrived, I explained that Camre was acting very weird. He examined her and then sent a psychiatrist to evaluate her, since he thought she might be suffering from post-partum psychosis. Now, I could have told them that Camre wasn't like Camre at all, but because I still didn't know what was going on, I agreed to let the psychiatrist examine her.

The psychiatrist was abrupt and aloof. He sent all of us out of the room and examined her for less than five minutes. When he came out, he pronounced that she was indeed suffering from post-partum psychosis. He explained she was incoherent because she was trying to not think about what had happened. Basically he said that the stress of labor and delivery had made her crazy. That didn't sound right to me, but before I could ask any questions, he took off. Her parents and I were shuttled into a separate room where we met with a behavior therapist. She told us that post-partum depression/psychosis was extremely serious. It could last for days or it could last for years. We barely had time to wrap our heads around the idea that Camre had lost her mind when the therapist said that the medical team had decided she should be transferred to a psych ward in another hospital.

I shook my head. "No, that's not going to happen." The therapist looked shocked, but I continued. "Before we accept that Camre is crazy, we need to get a second opinion." She reluctantly agreed and we went back to Camre's room.

By this time, Camre was fully conscious, but completely out of it mentally. She was still hooked up to oxygen and IVs, but they had placed her into a wheelchair because someone had the bright idea that maybe if she saw Gavin, she would snap out of her psychosis. Now all of this is taking place in the middle of the night, about 3 a.m. We were exhausted but we agreed to see what would happen. They wheeled her down to the NICU and over to Gavin's incubator.

"This is your son," I said. She just stared blankly. "Here," I took her hand and guided it into the incubator so she could touch Gavin. "This is your boy." She began to pat him gently, but it was clear she had no idea where she was or what she was doing. She never was belligerent or angry; she

59

was always like "okay, whatever" when we asked her to do something, so she stroked Gavin, but it was obvious she had no connection with him. The medical team continued to think it was merely post-partum psychosis, but her parents and I knew that it was much more than that. Camre had been so excited about becoming a mom, we knew that the sight of her baby would have brought her around if that had been the right diagnosis.

After it became apparent that seeing Gavin wasn't going to help, the medical team had to decide where to put her. Because they thought she was crazy rather than severely ill, they decided to take her to the labor and delivery floor and treat her like a new mom. I wasn't comfortable with that decision, but I was still assuming that the doctors knew what they were doing. As the nurse wheeled her to her room, Camre babbled constantly. None of it made any sense.

"Is she always like this?" the nurse asked, as Camre held her nonsense conversation with her hand. "Space monkey. Frog. Fishing. Let's go. Yeah."

"No," I said. "This isn't normal. I don't know what's going on but something is seriously wrong." We entered her new room, where an older guy, a volunteer of some sort, was sitting. I felt the hairs on the back of my neck rise.

"Who's that?" I demanded. "What's his background?"

"He's here to watch over her, make sure she doesn't hurt herself," the nurse explained.

At that point, something snapped in me. I knew then that I had to be Camre's advocate. I could no longer rely on the medical team to direct us. I needed to take charge of the situation. I might not be able to fix it, but I sure as heck wasn't going to sit around letting someone else make all the decisions.

"That isn't happening," I said emphatically. "That isn't going to work. I'm not leaving her with him. Either I sit here with her and you get rid of whoever that guy is, or you can take her back upstairs. With the way she is behaving, I don't think she needs to be in labor and delivery. She needs to go back to ICU and we need to figure out what's going on." I stood in front of the wheelchair; I wasn't going to let the nurse take Camre one step farther.

The nurse looked at me and nodded. "I totally agree with you. Something's not right. She doesn't belong here."

"I know. It's very obvious. I don't even know why we are doing this. Get her out of here."

We wheeled her out of the room with the creepy man and headed back to ICU. After a few tense minutes, we got Camre settled back in a bed. I resumed my place in the uncomfortable chair by her bedside.

I was groggy and exhausted when morning finally came. All I could think was, *Can someone just figure out what is going on?* During the morning, I went back and forth between Camre and Gavin. I couldn't just leave him alone down there in NICU and I couldn't leave her alone up there in ICU. I was trying to be there for both of them, because I knew I had to be.

The next thing the doctors tried was giving her an antidepressant, because they were still thinking she was depressed from the birth trauma. After that things went south—quick. She became catatonic. Her body went completely rigid and her temperature shot up to 105. Now a temperature of 105 is really serious. If she hadn't already had brain damage, she could have had more when her temperature got that high. At that point, I had more than enough. We'd been there for five days with no real answers. Camre was getting sicker by the hour. We didn't know if she was going to make it. Her parents and I decided that she needed to be transported to a different hospital with a more sophisticated neurology unit where they could do the kind of tests that were needed to figure out what had happened. We called the University of Michigan Medical School hospital and explained the situation. They had room for her, so they sent their life-flight helicopter team to pick her up.

It wasn't long afterwards that this tall, muscular dude in a flight suit walked into the ICU and owned the place. It was clear he was a total bad ass. I half-expected him to pull off aviator glasses like Tom Cruise in *Top Gun*. As he glanced around the room, he began barking orders. "I need this. I need that. You need to do that." People literally jumped to follow his directions. Within a few minutes, he had Camre hooked up to the equipment they needed to safely transport her. As his team was wheeling her to the private elevator that led to the helicopter deck, he came over to me and looked me directly in the eye.

"You the fiancé?"

"Yes, I am."

He nodded. "I've got it under control. She's in good hands now."

Uncertain Answers

I could hear the whirr of the helicopter as it prepared for takeoff from the floor above us. I walked over to the window and waited until I could see it make its way into the distance. I felt a surge of relief, not just knowing that she was in safe hands, but that we would finally be able to get some answers.

I knew I had to tell Gavin what had happened. I rode the public elevator downstairs to the NICU. After I scrubbed, I leaned over his incubator and touched his tiny fingers. "Hey, buddy. Your mom is at another hospital now. They are going to find out what happened to her and take care of her. Don't worry. Everything's going to be all right. I love you so much and we are all going to get through this." Talking to him, but talking to me. As I held his hand, one of the nurses I had gotten to know came up.

"Hi there. How's Camre?" I explained that she was being transported to a different hospital for some more sophisticated testing. "I hope they can find some answers," she said.

"Me, too," I said. "Me, too."

It was hard to leave Gavin, but I knew I needed to be with Camre, too. On the forty-five minute drive to the University of Michigan, I thought about the future. It was becoming clear to me that I was going to need a crash course in Baby 101 before we took Gavin home. Fortunately, I still had a few weeks before that would happen, but I was still overwhelmed by the thought. *How was I going to take care of a baby, visit Camre, and still work?* At that point, I just told myself, "You've got this. It's all going to work out."

Over the next few days, I divvied up my time between learning all I could about taking care of a newborn from the NICU nurses, visiting Camre, taking care of the dogs—by now we had two—and the house, and all the other regular stuff that has to be done. The doctors at U of M were running all kinds of tests on Camre and while we still didn't have any answers, I felt confident that they were doing all that could be done.

One afternoon, as I was driving to see Camre, I got a call from the hospital. They told me that Camre had pulled out all the staples from her C-section and was in emergency surgery. By the time I got to see her, I was horrified to learn that they had to put her in restraints to keep her from pulling out the new staples. Looking at the love of my life, the mother of our son, tied to a hospital bed, babbling incoherently, was almost the breaking point. *What more could possibly happen?* I wondered. *How much more can we take?*

But the worst was yet to come.

When I came the next day, I saw her parents in the hall outside her room. Her mom had an unusually tense expression on her face, but I chalked it up to fatigue. Lord knows we were all exhausted. I leaned up against the wall, propping one foot off the floor, getting myself together before I went in to see Camre.

"How's she doing? Is there any news?"

"Steve," her mom said softly. Her eyes were filled with tears.

I felt my throat constrict. "What is it? What did they tell you?"

"Not a lot," she said, "but they told us that they think she has irreversible brain damage."

"What does that mean?"

"She doesn't know who I am," her mom said. "She doesn't know who you are or who Gavin is. She doesn't know any of us and probably never will."

I broke down sobbing. I had suspected that Camre might have had something wrong with her brain, but I never expected to hear that she would never recover. Her mom reached out and hugged me, but I was beyond comforting. I had never imagined that the worst could be this bad. To be honest, I didn't want to accept it. I was in complete denial.

64

Once I got myself together, I walked into Camre's room. "Hey, Cam, how you doing?" I tried to sound as normal as possible. She didn't acknowledge me. She didn't even look up. I'm guessing she thought that I was just another doctor or nurse. Camre's eyes wandered about the room. I had thought that her forgetfulness was the result of medication, but I never expected it to be permanent. With trying to sort out this news, it was too painful for me to stay very long, so I gave her a kiss on the forehead. Her dad had come back into her room and we walked out together to the hall.

In that moment I made my decision. I was never going to give up on Camre. It wasn't going to happen. I was going to be there for her for the rest of her life. I turned to her dad and said, "Your daughter might not know who I am today. She might not know who I am tomorrow. But she will in the future. I'm not going anywhere, ever."

As soon as I said those words, I knew I had to be with Gavin. I drove straight to the hospital where Gavin was. I knew I had to see him, to make sure that he really was okay. I remember driving down the expressway and I just lost it. I hit the wall. I was sobbing and clenching the steering wheel, screaming in my head, "Why? Why did this happen? How could this have happened?"

I entered the NICU as usual and scrubbed up. I didn't say anything to the nurses. I just walked over to Gavin. I was finally able to hold him, so I scooped him up in my arms. One thing I remember about that day is that he was wearing a bright orange cap. Preemies have to wear hats to keep warm, but this one was a toque, as the Canadians call ski hats. The top of his little head was completely hidden, but his bright eyes knowingly looked up at me. I rocked him back and forth as I explained what was happening with his mom.

"Hey, buddy, it's not good. Your mom has brain damage and it's bad. But don't worry. Our family is going to be okay. We are going to get through this. I'm not sure exactly what is going to happen, but we are going to make it together." I kissed his forehead and kept saying, "It's going to be okay. Don't worry." I'm sure I was talking to myself as much as I was talking to him when I said, "I've got this. We can handle it." The nurses kept coming up to me, asking how Camre was. Finally, I shared with one of them that she had a traumatic brain injury and had lost all her memory.

"Just doesn't know who she is or who I am or that we had a child."

"Oh my gosh," the nurse said. "Are you serious?"

"Yeah," I said. "I wish I weren't but it's true."

"That's unbelievable," the nurse said. "I'm so sorry. She touched me lightly on the shoulder. "If there is anything we can do to help …"

"Well," I said. "I guess I'm going to be taking care of this tiny baby when he goes home. I don't know the first thing about babies, so give me all the pointers you can."

I've said before that the NICU nurses are the best and they really are. For the rest of the time Gavin was in the hospital, they taught me how to feed and change him. They explained to me how to hold him. They showed me how to bathe him and how to burb him. I can't begin to say what a blessing they all were. They would log in then all take turns helping me figure out how to be both mom and dad to Gavin. One thing strikes me when I look at the pictures is that Gavin was just a perfect, miniature baby with an amazing grip. I still marvel that he could be so strong and so healthy, even though he was so tiny. But I never could have done it without the help of those nurses. They were angels. They helped me gain the confidence that I really could take him home and take care of him.

By this time about three weeks had passed since Camre had the brain injury and Gavin was born. The neurosurgeon had explained as much as they knew about it—that she had become eclamptic and suffered loss of oxygen to the brain, resulting in long-term, perhaps permanent, memory loss. It was clear to me that's what happened, because she never knew me when I came to see her. However, I'd still talk to her as if she were Camre. I told her that I would always be there for her and told her to be strong because she was going to get better.

Once they figured out what had happened, Camre was downgraded from ICU to a standard room. She was on medication to prevent more seizures, but she was off all the other drugs. Almost immediately they began the kind of physical and occupational therapy that they give to stroke victims to see if that could help. Soon she was able to get up and walk around. It didn't take too long for her to begin making more sense when she talked, but she still didn't have any memory for more than a couple of seconds. She couldn't remember eating even if the food was still in front of her. She didn't recognize her parents or me. That was one of the hardest things. Every time I came in the room, I was a stranger. To her credit, she wasn't afraid. As I've said, she is one of the bravest, strongest women I know. However, it was clear that she didn't have a clue who anyone was and she certainly didn't have any idea that she was a mom.

After about another week, they decided to release her. Although Gavin was going to stay in the hospital another few weeks until his lungs were fully developed and his feeding tube was removed, I knew I couldn't take Camre back to our house. It wasn't that I didn't want to take care of her. I would have gladly done anything for her, but I was in a tough spot. I had used up all my vacation and sick leave, so I had to go back to work in order to pay my bills. Her parents and I decided that she would stay at their home until we got things figured out.

Coming Home

Once Camre was back at her mom's, she began to make rapid strides on the physical front. It is typical of her strength and determination. Even when she didn't know what was going on, she was determined to do as much as she could for herself. Soon she was able to walk and talk, although she still needed help with finding the bathroom, that kind of thing. If you didn't know something was wrong, you couldn't have told it from the way she looked. But if you were with her for even a few minutes, you'd know that something was way off. For the first couple of days she was at her parents, I would go to work and then come over to see her in the afternoon.

A typical conversation would go like:

"Hi, Camre. It's me, Steve."

She would just stare at me.

"How was your day?"

"Okay."

"You want to go see your son?"

More staring.

"I'm going to the hospital to see Gavin, now. You want to come with me?"

"No, I'm good." It was clear she had no idea who I was or why I was talking about her having had a son. At this point, her mother would sometimes intervene. "Camre, this is Steve. He's your fiancé. He's the father of your son. You should go with him."

Most of the time Camre would respond with a smile. She never was hostile or angry, but she was determined. "No, I'm good. No, I don't want to go," she would say with a cheerful grin. Her parents didn't want me to push her and I didn't want to either, so I'd leave her and go see Gavin. But I knew that this arrangement couldn't last forever.

By the third day, I put my foot down. "You're going with me," I told her. "You need to see your son." I want to emphasize that I wasn't trying to be mean or bossy. It's just that I knew I had to do all I could to get my Camre to come back. I wanted to help her, not enable her. Just letting her sit on the couch at her mom's wasn't helping her at all.

We drove to the hospital. All the way, she was cheerful and smiling, but she didn't have a clue where we were going. We went into the NICU. I showed her how to scrub up and then introduced her to the nurses. We walked over to the incubator where Gavin was sleeping.

"Camre, this is our son. This is Gavin."

She peered down at him. "Gavin? That's a nice name."

"Yep, you helped pick it out." She smiled again.

The nurses and I decided that it might be helpful if she could hold him. Remember that she never was violent or destructive, so we didn't have any worries that she might have hurt Gavin. The nurses slid over a comfortable chair and put Gavin in her arms.

"Camre, this is Gavin. He's your son."

She looked at him and touched his cheek. "Whose baby is this?"

"He's your baby."

"I have a baby?"

"Yes, you have a baby. His name is Gavin."

"Oh, okay." She looked down at him again. "Whose baby is this?"

"He's our son. He's your baby."

"I have a baby?"

"Yes, you have a baby."

"Oh, okay." She looked around "Whose baby is this?"

"He's your baby."

"Oh, okay. What's his name?"

"Gavin, his name is Gavin."

She held him for a couple more minutes and then looked up at me. "Whose baby is this?" For as long as we were there, the conversation never changed. This kind of questioning went on for weeks, even months. I will admit it was both heartbreaking and frustrating, but I clung to every bit of progress. The one thing that gave me encouragement was when she began to respond to her own name. After days of constant reminding, when I'd speak to her, she finally would look up and sometimes she would say, "I'm Camre, right?" Just to have her be able to understand that much was a huge thing.

The next big step came when she began to recognize me. At first, she had no idea who I was. I was a complete stranger each time she saw me. Then one night after we visited Gavin, she looked at me and said, "I think I know you. You are around here every day, aren't you?"

"Yes. I'm your fiancé."

"Okay, I know you are here all the time, but I can't remember your name. Tell me the first letter. Maybe I can remember it."

"S."

"Scott?"

"Nope."

"Sam?"

"Nope."

"Steve?"

"Right! You've got it. I'm Steve."

The same thing would happen with Gavin. We'd go to the hospital, she'd hold him and say to me, "This is my baby, right?"

70

"Right, that's your baby."

"What's his name? No, don't tell me. What letter does it start with?"

"G."

"G? G? Greg?"

"No, it's Gavin."

"Oh yeah, that's right. He's Gavin. And I'm Camre, right?

"That's right. You've got it."

Even now it's difficult to explain what it was like. At times it was almost as if her brain were waking up, but then she could go right back into blankness. However, each time she made the littlest bit of progress, I was encouraged. It gave me hope that one day she would be able to be the mom she had always dreamed of, even if that day was a long ways off.

The next ten days were brutal. Most mornings I would get up a couple of hours before I had to go to work and visit Gavin. I went to see him every lunch hour. Every night after work, I'd stop by Camre's parents and say, "Okay, honey, let's go see our son." Sometimes she would come right along, but most of the time she would be very reluctant. Finally, her parents began to push her as well. Her mom would say, "Camre, you have to go with Steve now." She'd cooperate, but she never could remember why she had to go with me.

One evening Gavin was sleeping and Camre and I were sitting on the couch. I could barely keep my eyes open, I was so tired. I had just explained to Camre who I was and who Gavin was for what seemed like the hundredth time in ten minutes. Each time she would smile, say "Oh, okay," and the next second she would ask again. All of sudden, she turned and looked me directly in the eyes.

"I don't know who you are," she said, "but I know I love you."

In that moment, all my worries vanished. I knew then that despite all we had gone through and all that we faced in the future, everything was going to be okay.

Baby Makes Three

On November 11, just about a month after he was born, Gavin was finally big enough to come home. His original due date had been November 27, so he was still tiny but he no longer needed around the clock nursing care.

It was a day that I had been waiting for and dreading at the same time. While Gavin was in the hospital, I knew he was safe, but when he came home, all that responsibility was going to fall on me. The NICU nurses assured me that I was better prepared than most new dad (and moms), but it was still nerve-racking.

That day Camre came with me to the hospital. We parked my white Silverado crew cab with the brand-new car seat in the back and walked into the NICU. We stopped at the scrub station and I realized that this was the last time that I was going to have to scrub up before holding Gavin.

"You ready to take your baby home?" the nurse asked.

"As ready as I can be," I laughed. "But I still have a million questions." I knew the entire job of parenting was going to be on my shoulders so we sat down and went over everything I could think of one more time—everything from changing diapers to figuring out if he were sick. I checked and double-checked how to mix his formula and how much to feed him at a time. I made sure I knew how to hold up his head so it didn't wobble. I made the nurses show me how to bathe him. Finally, the nurse said the heart-stopping words, "Okay, you're ready to go."

Now all this time, Camre was with me, but she really wasn't paying much attention. I'm not sure if she really understood that Gavin was coming home with us. As the nurses tucked Gavin into the car seat, I felt like we were baby birds flying the nest and going out on our own. At the last minute, I put the little monkey hat from the shower on his head. Camre smiled at the sight, even though I knew she didn't remember seeing it before.

I was smiling from ear-to-ear as I walked out of that hospital with Gavin in his car seat and Camre by my side. Yet my heart was racing, too, because I knew that we all faced a tough road ahead. Nevertheless, I wasn't going to let it faze me. I believe that God only gives you what you can handle, but apparently he thinks I can handle a lot. So I put my faith in God and moved forward. *You've got this,* I told myself as I put Gavin in the back seat. *You can handle it. You can do this. Just take it one day at a time.*

I made sure he was secure about fifty million times and tripled-checked everything else. Camre buckled herself in next to him and we began the drive home. My dad always used to tell me that he drove about five miles an hour when he brought me home from the hospital and in the back of my mind the thought kicked in, *Oh wow, I'm the dad now.* I white-knuckled the steering wheel all the way to our house. I drove a little faster than five miles an hour, but not much. Camre was with us, physically, but she wasn't there mentally. She had no idea where we were going and I'm pretty sure she didn't understand that Gavin was her baby yet.

We drove down our driveway and parked in front of the house. I had hung a "It's a Boy! Welcome Gavin" sign on the front. I pointed it out to Camre. Once again she smiled, but it was clear she didn't understand the meaning. I got out, opened the back door of the truck so she could get out, and then picked up Gavin. We walked directly through the kitchen to the nursery. I took him out of the car seat as Camre watched and then I started showing him the house.

"Hey, buddy. Look, this is your new house. Welcome home. This is going to be your bedroom. This is the living room. See, it looks right out on the lake." All the time, Camre followed us, but she didn't really say anything. Once we finished the tour, I helped Camre sit in the rocking chair we had and put Gavin in her arms. She held him close and began to rock him back and forth gently.

I was struck by how surreal the moment was. I had just brought my son home. My fiancée had no memory of giving birth. She didn't even really understand that she was holding her own baby, but she was smiling and rocking him. From the outside, it looked like we were just a normal, everyday family, but we weren't normal at all.

A little later in the day, Camre's parents came over. They visited for a few minutes before taking Camre home with them. That had been the plan all along, but when they left, it was harder than I expected. I watched them pull out of the driveway and realized it was just Gavin and me. I was on my own, alone with a newborn. As I headed to the kitchen to fix him a bottle, I said, "Don't worry, buddy. I've got this." I think I was talking to myself as much as I was talking to him.

Camre's parents brought her over to spend the next day, which was a Sunday, with Gavin and me. When they all went home, we were alone again that second night. I had to go to work on Monday, so my mom took a week's vacation to help us out. The first week, she would come to my house in the morning and watch Gavin during the day. After work, I'd either go pick up Camre and bring her to the house or her parents would bring her over. Then, at night, she would go back to her parents' house.

At that time and for a long time afterwards, she thought that her parents' house was her house. She was uncomfortable and maybe even a little scared to spend the night with me because I was essentially a stranger. While it was hard, I understood. It was like she was going on a first date every single time she saw me. A first date with the ever-present possibility of a sleepover. After a couple of weeks, I decided that this wasn't the healthiest arrangement for any of us. It wasn't so much the need for intimacy as it was the need to begin creating a more normal family routine. Soon I realized that the longer the situation went on as it was, the harder it was going to be on all of us to make the change. One evening, when I picked her up, I broke the news to the family.

"Camre is coming home with me and she is going to stay with us at night."

"Are you sure about that?" her mom asked. Her mom had become very protective of her daughter.

"Yes. I'm sure. I know that Camre wanted to be a mom more than anything, so we've got to start living as a family as much as we can."

"But Camre can't stay alone with Gavin during when you are working. She can't take care of him. She can't take care of herself!"

"That's true, but what I was thinking was that Camre would spend the evenings and nights with me and then Gavin and she could come to your house during the day. If you are willing to do that, then they'll be safe until I can take care of them."

Her mom was all on board with that plan. "Camre, I agree with Steve. I think it would be a good idea for you to start spending the nights at your house. He is your fiancé. You need to be a family." I'm not sure if Camre really understood what all that meant, but she was always cheerful and agreeable, so she didn't object. That afternoon, we came home to spend our first night together as a family. We have been together ever since.

New Normal

The way our new normal worked was that I would load up Camre and Gavin about six in the morning and drive them to her parents' house. I'd go to work and they'd stay there. Then at night, I'd pick them up, come home, feed Gavin, fix dinner, go to bed, and start it all over in the morning. Except that I rarely got more than a couple of hours of sleep a night. Gavin wasn't a great sleeper for the first couple of years. Even if Camre had gotten up with him, she wouldn't have known what to do. So I was the one who had to do it. Sometimes I'd get so desperate, I'd put him and Camre into the car at 1 a.m. and drive them around town to get him to go to sleep. Other times, I'd put him in his car seat on the dryer and let the noise and shaking soothe him.

I never want to sound like I'm complaining because I would do it all again in a minute. But it was still challenging for all of us. It took Camre quite a while to get comfortable staying all night because she couldn't remember having been there from one day to the next. For the first couple of years, when I'd pick her and Gavin up at her parents' house, she would ask, "Where are we going?"

"We're going home."

"We just left my home."

"No, that was your parents' home. You live with me in Linden."

"Oh, okay." We'd drive into our driveway and she'd ask, "Where are we?"

"We're at home."

"This is my home?"

"Yes, this is our home."

"Oh. I live here?"

"Yes, you live here."

Some days were a little better than others, but most of the time she was either confused or oblivious to what was going on. During that time, my major goal, besides making sure that Gavin was taken care of, was to keep Camre involved in being a mom. One of the saddest things for me was that she never had the opportunity to just be a mom, to do ordinary mom things, so I would have her with me whenever I took care of Gavin. For instance, I must have showed her how to change a diaper a thousand times. Sometimes when I handed her a diaper, she would just stare at it. Other times she'd put it on backward or try to slide it on. I also wanted her to have the bonding experience of feeding Gavin. I'd get the bottle heated up, sit her down in the rocking chair, put a rag on her shoulder, and bring Gavin to her. I'd have to show her every time how to put the bottle in his mouth. Then I'd show her how to hold him and burb him. I was a dad playing both mom and dad/fiancé/teacher/caregiver right out of the gate. At the time, I didn't allow myself to think too much about the future. I would just wake up in the morning and say, "Okay, Steve, you've got this. You can do it."

I've said that I marked each little step of progress. One of the biggest moments came when I realized that Camre understood that she was Gavin's mom. It wasn't dramatic, but one day I noticed that she finally "got it." I was so proud of her and yet I knew that the next day she wouldn't remember how much it had meant to me.

During that first year or so, Camre was both like a child and an adult at the same time. For instance, one time she said the word "shit" and immediately added, "Oh, don't tell my parents I said that!" Yet, she retained the sarcastic streak that she always had. Once someone asked her how I was doing as a dad and she said, with a big grin, "Oh, I guess he's doing the best he can."

She always had a million questions. One day she asked me, "How do I get out of our house?"

"You go out the front door over there."

78

She rolled her eyes at me. "No, how do I leave here?"

"You've got to go up the driveway. Why, do you want to go somewhere?"

"I just want to know. If I go up the driveway, which way is my parents' house?"

"Right."

"I would turn right?"

"Yeah, you'd turn right."

"So how do I get out of the house?"

She wanted to know how we'd met, where we'd met, when Gavin was born, when her birthday was. I'd tell her and in the next moment, she'd ask the same questions all over. Gradually, very gradually, her brain began to make new connections, but that made things harder as well. She began to realize that she had a brain injury, but she couldn't remember what that meant. We were trapped in a vicious circle of remembering that she couldn't remember, and then forgetting that she remembered.

I've been asked if I got angry. My family assures me that I never got angry, but I know I got frustrated. I wasn't frustrated at first, but when you've told a person the same thing a thousand, two thousand times and they ask the same question over and over, it's hard not to get frustrated. I knew that being frustrated at her wasn't going to help, so I would just let it go. I'd say to myself, "It's okay, Steve. It's going to be okay. Don't dwell on it. Let it go." If I could, I'd go on the deck for a couple of minutes, play with the dogs, take some deep breaths. When I'd come back in, I'd be ready to show Camre how to change a diaper one more time. If I couldn't leave her and Gavin for even a second, I'd just remind myself that this was happening, this was real. I was committed to Camre. I wasn't going to let her live this life—our life—without me being a part of it.

About a year into our new normal, when Camre began occupational therapy on a regular basis, things got a little easier for all of us. In occupational therapy, she learned to do things most of us take for granted—like going grocery shopping or doing the dishes. It took a long time and lots of practice, but in time, Camre has relearned many of those skills. We write everything down and keep notes all over the house, but she has come so far from those early months I sometimes can't believe it.

Looking back, Camre today is the same person she always was but, at the same time, she is incredibly different. As she was gradually recovering, I often had to wing it a lot. She looked and sounded like the woman I loved, but she wasn't that woman anymore. Even though the doctors had told us in medical terms what had happened, no one really understood what it all meant. We literally had to take it one day at a time.

Just when we thought that we were making some real progress, I got a call at work from her mom. Camre had had a seizure and was on her way to the hospital. From that point on, Camre started having grand mal seizures once every two or three weeks. Gradually, they increased until she was having a couple of seizures every day or every other day. They would come without warning. We might be out shopping and she'd begin to seize. We might be watching TV and she would seize. We never knew when it would happen. Epilepsy was a major setback and a major change in our plans. We had gotten to the place where I could let Camre and Gavin be together for a few minutes while I went to the bathroom or whatever. Or I could go on the deck and watch them through the window. I did that so that both of them could have some time alone to bond with each other. But once she began to have seizures, I was constantly thinking, *What if she falls on the baby? What if she hurts herself?* Every worst-case scenario raced through my mind.

I've said that I've always had faith that things were going to be okay, so I really had to exercise that faith when the seizures started. I knew that Camre missed her independence, so sometimes I would make sure that Gavin was safe and go into another room, even if it was just for a minute or two. I never really could leave them, though. If I had to go to the grocery store or if I had to go outside to do yard work, I had to take them with me.

Camre's epilepsy has been an ongoing battle that continues to this day. Just when we thought we were letting up on doctors' appointments, we started having a whole new set of doctors to see. They tried many different medications, some of which worked better than others, but none of them actually eliminated the seizures. Because of her brain injury, none of the current surgeries that are available is an option, so eventually she had a VNS implant.

A VNS, or vagus nerve stimulator, is a stopwatch-sized pacemaker implanted under the skin of the chest. It's programmed to send an electronic signal to the brain in a programmed cycle, such as thirty seconds on and five minutes off. This signal helps to correct the electrical stimuli that causes seizures. It can also be activated if a seizure begins by swiping a magnet over the implantation site. While the VNS isn't a cure, it has cut the number of seizures Camre has in half or more. Instead of happening every week or even more frequently, she now can go a couple of weeks. But seizures are still a major part of our lives. I estimate that she had three- or four-hundred seizures, maybe even more, in the first six years.

Nevertheless, we both considered epilepsy just another hurdle to overcome. It was just another thing for us to get through together. We started doing "regular" family things, like holidays and vacations. Even though Camre wasn't comfortable out in public with people she didn't know, she was able to begin to relax and even enjoy life a little bit with our close friends and relatives who understood the situation. After a couple of years of this "new normal," where Gavin and Camre spent weekdays with her parents and nights and weekends at our home, I began to think about the future. Even though I had made a lifetime commitment never to leave Camre, we weren't married. It dawned on me that while her parents had always allowed me to make the decisions regarding her care, if something happened to them, the state could step in. There was no guarantee that I would be allowed to be her protector for the rest of her life. I kicked myself that I hadn't married her long before now, when things were more complicated. It's one thing to be a fiancé, but it's another to be a husband. I decided that had to change, for my sake as much as for Camre.

I Do

I decided to ask her to marry me again before we started talking about a wedding. I told her mom and dad that I wanted to get re-engaged and they gave their blessing. One issue was the ring. Camre wore her engagement ring all the time. I couldn't take it off her finger and then give it right back to her. She'd never understand what was happening. Her mom reminded me that early on in our relationship, I had given Camre a promise ring, which was still in her jewelry box. I immediately knew it would be ideal.

My mom always has a big Fourth of July party, so exactly one year after our first engagement, in my mom's yard, I got down on one knee, and proposed again in front of all our family. It's odd, but I was more nervous the second time than the first. I couldn't guarantee that she wouldn't say, "No, I'm good." Fortunately, she said "yes" once again.

We decided to wait a couple more years while Camre continued the slow, but steady, process of reclaiming herself. I wanted her to be absolutely sure that she wanted to be married as much as I did. The last thing I would ever do is try to take advantage of her condition. Our everyday life settled into its new normal. She and Gavin continued to spend the days at her mom's and the nights and weekends with me. Camre went to occupational therapy and practiced the skills she was learning. Gavin did all the things a little boy should do, like learning to walk and talk and be a kid. Sometimes Camre looks at pictures from that time and tells me how much she wishes she could remember. I tell her that the past doesn't matter as much as today. I tell her we've always taken it one day at a time and that's how we always will do it.

Finally, when Camre was able to process and completely understand what getting married meant and how it was different from being engaged, it was time to plan our wedding. She still didn't have more than a few hours, or a day at best, worth of memory for events, but she was doing remarkably well with things that were encoded in her rote memory. With some supervision, she could cook simple foods, do laundry, feed the dogs. (Today, she can remember what happened a few days ago and we are hopeful that will only continue to increase with time.)

Anyway, by the time we were ready to get married, she was much more aware of her surroundings, so she was able to give input into the plans. However, we could never have done it without our families. It was all family on deck for the wedding. Without their help, I'd still be trying to get it together.

One thing we both knew we wanted was to be married in our backyard, which overlooked the lake. It was where we had started our relationship. It was where we had gotten engaged the first time. It was where we brought Gavin home. It was the perfect place for us to take the next step.

I know a lot of guys aren't all that involved in wedding planning, but I had no choice. One thing I wanted to do was to have Redwood Lodge, the place we went on our first date, cater the wedding. Another thing that was important was to have her mom make the cake. Her mom had owned and operated a cake-decorating business, so I knew that was one thing that had to happen. I had a surprise planned, too, but I didn't let anyone know about that.

Camre was aware that she was getting married, not because she actually remembered the planning, but because over the six months of preparation, we talked about it every day. A typical conversation would go something like:

"We're getting married, right?"

"Yep."

"When are we getting married?"

"September 12th."

"Oh, okay."

"Who's coming to our wedding?"

"All of our family and friends."

"Where is the wedding going to be? No, don't tell me. It's going to be here, in our yard, right?

"Right. Here in our yard."

We knew we wanted to get married at an altar, so a couple of days before the wedding, my brother and I built one with rustic round logs and a sheer, white fabric draped over the top. We got all the family involved the day before, putting lights in the trees and decorating the yard. The catering company set up a tent for a reception with heaters—just in case—and a dance area.

Camre and her mom had picked out a dress that Camre absolutely loved. We had decided on a white and gold theme for the wedding, so I chose tan slacks with a white shirt and gold suspenders. Gavin had a matching outfit, so he was dressed like me, even thought he still looked more like his mom.

Camre had gone to her parents' home the night before, so Gavin and I had one last night alone. The morning of the wedding, I cooked him breakfast and talked about what was going to happen.

"Mommy and Daddy are going to get married," I explained. "Right now, Mommy has a different last name, but after today, all of us are going to be Curtos—we'll have the same name."

"Yeah," he said between bites. "And lots of people are going to come, right?"

"Right. And right after Mommy and Daddy get married, we are going to pour sand together to show how we are family."

"Can we do it right now?"

I laughed. "No, buddy. We have to wait. We'll tell you when it's time to mix the sand."

Around noon, my mom took Gavin so I could have a few hours to myself. I checked on the wedding prep, then walked down to the shore of the lake. I took a stick and wrote in the sand, "Steve and Camre, 2015." I stood for awhile, feeling the warm fall air and thinking over all that had happened the past few years. But there was no time to waste. I went back into the house to get dressed and wait for my bride to arrive.

As the caterers finished and the guests started to arrive, the sky clouded up and a light mist began to fall. It was a little disappointing that our wedding wasn't going to take place on one of those incredible fall days that make Michigan so beautiful, but I wasn't going to let anything—especially not a little mist—dampen our experience. We'd figure something out.

Of course, it wouldn't be a wedding without at least one little mishap. I had an issue with one of my suspenders, so Camre's sister made an emergency run to the store to get a new one. While I was waiting for the new suspenders, the mist threatened to turn to rain. The wedding was scheduled for 3 p.m., so I made an executive decision to push it back 30 minutes in the hopes that the weather might break. Besides, there was no rush. Camre was still at her parents' house. Finally, the time arrived. I walked down to the altar to wait for Camre. After all that we had been through, all that we had to do to get to this moment, we were finally getting married! I kicked myself again that we hadn't done this a lot sooner, but when they opened the door and Camre stepped out on our deck, something magical happened. The clouds suddenly parted. The rain stopped. A beam of sunlight landed directly on her. She was smiling that magical smile that always puts a catch in my throat. Tears dripped down my face as she walked toward me on the white carpet we had laid on the grass. I felt like God was giving us his blessing, but maybe he was just telling me, "About time, Steve!"

In addition to the sand mixing, Gavin was going to hand us our rings. When the time arrived for him to come forward, he tripped over the white carpet and sort of fell at our feet. Fortunately, he began to laugh, so everyone else laughed, too. He helped me put the ring on his mom's finger, but then he refused to go sit back down. He put his arms around both of our legs and just stood there with us. Eventually, his granddad came to get him, but he stayed as close as he could. I think he knew how important this day was for all of us.

Then we said our own vows. I wanted to speak from the heart instead of reciting some formula. I told Camre how much I loved her and that I would be with her for life. She was still feeling a little uncomfortable speaking in public, so she said something simple like, "I love you." We held hands as we pledged to be together for the rest of our lives.

Then it was the time Gavin had been waiting for—mixing sand. "Over the Rainbow" was playing as Camre, Gavin, and I poured layers of white and tan sand into one jar to represent our finally being united as a permanent family. While it was a special moment of the day, Camre doesn't remember it. She doesn't remember anything about our wedding. I think that is one of the most difficult things for her—not to be able to remember her wedding day. She watches the video, but she says it's like watching a movie. The one positive is that while she might not be able to remember the events, she does remember how happy she was and how much it meant to her. The memories aren't there, but the emotions are.

Right after the minister introduced us as husband and wife, my final surprise was revealed. As we raised our hands in celebration, fireworks exploded from a boat on the lake. All during the wedding, the guests saw this boat floating back and forth quite near the shore. Some of them thought it was just a rude stalker trying to spy on our wedding, but it actually was my neighbor. I had arranged for him to set off fireworks at the conclusion of the ceremony. Since the first time Camre and I got engaged it was during Fourth of July fireworks, I thought it would be fitting to come full circle to have fireworks on our wedding day. Hey, I've admitted I have a romantic streak.

The rest of the afternoon was spent taking mandatory wedding pictures and then celebrating into the night with family and friends. We ended the evening with a bonfire, which only seemed fitting. When everyone had left, including Gavin, who went to stay with his grandparents, Camre walked into the house. The next morning we were going to take a short honeymoon to Mackinac Island on Lake Huron and she wanted to be rested. "I'll be right there," I said. "I just want to make sure the fire is out." I stirred the embers to ashes then joined Camre—the love of my life—my wife.

Dancing into the Future

The leaves crunched underfoot as Gavin and I walked to our backyard. Today, we live in the most idyllic spot I can imagine. We have twenty-two acres on a creek. It's like a wildlife preserve with deer, foxes, birds, squirrels, and all kinds of other critters. Our dogs think it's heaven. They aren't far off.

Gavin was chattering with excitement about target practice with his bow and arrow. We talked about safety measures. I reminded him that he must never shoot at anything other than a target.

He nodded his head, his eyes sparkling with enthusiasm. He fitted the arrow to the bow just as we had practiced and pulled back on the bowstring. The arrow flew toward the target at the edge of the woods, just nicking the bail of hay.

"Try again," I urged. He squared his shoulders and took aim. This time the arrow hit the target square and solid. "Good job!" I said as he turned to face me. Behind us, I heard Camre cheering. She was standing on the deck, clapping and giving Gavin a thumbs up.

"Keep trying," I said. "I'm going up on the deck to watch with Mom." He nodded and focused all his concentration on his aim.

I walked up the stairs to the deck and put my arm around Camre. "He's getting really good," she said.

"Yeah, he is. He's very strong for a little boy. He's come a long way since he shot his first arrow." Camre smiled, but I knew there was a hint of sadness. She didn't remember that day except for pictures. She didn't remember the scent of the fall air or the sight of the falling leaves. She didn't remember how we had to keep the dogs locked in the house for their own safety. But right now, in this moment, she knew that she was Gavin's mom and that she was very proud of him. "You've come a long way, too." She smiled again, that amazing smile that made me fall in love with her so long ago at Legends.

Gavin looked back at us and I gave him another thumbs up. "What's it like for you?" I asked. "I know I've watched how hard you work and have seen how far you've come, but what's it like for you now?"

Camre paused. "I never used to be able to remember anything. Now I can remember some of the things we did yesterday. When I wake up, I try to remember what I can, but mostly I just focus on the positive and begin the new day."

As always, I marvel at how articulate Camre is. If you didn't know that she had a severe brain injury and memory loss, you'd never know it when you first met her. She looks and sounds completely normal.

"So what do you remember about yesterday?" I asked. We had spent the day going to doctors' appointments, looking at new options for both her epilepsy and her brain injury.

"I remember that I couldn't have anything to drink and there you were, drinking coffee and telling me how it was the best coffee you've ever had and saying how sorry you were that I couldn't have any. I wanted to kick you in the butt, but you were driving and I didn't want to have an accident." She laughed. I'll admit that I had done that, but it wasn't to be mean. I try to keep our relationship as normal as possible. That means I tease her like I always have, although I try to be careful and not push her too far. My goal has always been to keep her moving forward, doing as much as she can by being there to support her.

Camre waved at Gavin as he went to gather his spent arrows. Most were firmly lodged in the target and one was nearly a bullseye. She looked somber. "I know what we did, but I can't remember the details. I can't remember when things happened or any of the details."

I've struggled to understand what it must be like for her. The closest I've been able to come is that it must be a little like after having major surgery. Anyone who has had surgery under a general anesthetic will probably know what I'm talking about. You know you had the surgery, but don't remember any of the details. You might even know that the doctors talked to you, but you don't remember what they said. I asked a friend with a lot of medical knowledge about that and she said that one of the drugs you get when you are under doesn't allow memories to be encoded in the brain. It is essentially a "forgetting" drug. Sometimes you can answer questions and follow directions, but the drug doesn't let the brain store any of those memories. It's used so that you don't remember any of the pain or other unpleasant things that can happen in surgery. That's the closest explanation I can come to understanding what it must be like for Camre. She "knows" things, but she can't "remember" them.

Gavin shot an arrow that landed short. "That's okay," Camre shouted. "Try again." She looked at me and said softly, "People assume that because I can't remember, I don't know things, but that's not the way it is. I know what I like to wear and what I like to eat …"

"That's for sure," I laughed. "Put a bowl of Cinnamon Chex cereal down and you'll probably steal it." She gave me one of "those" looks, but she didn't argue.

Gavin shouted. "Watch me, guys. I'm going to make a bullseye this time."

"I'll bet you will, buddy," I encouraged. As he repositioned his bow and arrows, I asked Camre, "What do you feel the most proud about? I am always so proud of you and all you've done, but what about you?"

"That you've stuck me with through all of this." She paused. "And I'm just so happy that Gavin came out the boy that he is. Just to have a little boy to give a kiss to each morning and each night. Sometimes you know that I get angry that this had to happen and I wonder why it had to happen. That's hard, especially as I get better and I realize how much I don't remember. That's hard

91

and frustrating." I hugged her closer as she continued. "There have been a lot of times when I think the brain injury took my life away, but it didn't."

"Yep, you're right about that. We still have our family and we have our life together."

Camre looked at me and smiled again. "I'm so proud of the love we share. The one thing that is always in my memory is the love I have and will always have for you." We shared a quick kiss before Gavin caught us. "It's like you always say," she went on. "We can do this. We just have to have hope and believe we can get through anything. We just have to keep going."

"Speaking of going," I said. "You guys have the dance tonight."

Camre nodded. I knew how important it was and is for Camre to be able to see just how much progress she has made and how far she has come. One of her greatest hopes is that one day she will be able to be a regular mom for Gavin. She often expresses her frustration at having to depend on me for everything. Once she said, "I just want to do regular, normal mom things. I just want to be a mom like every other mom." That evening was going to be one of the first tests for all of us. Gavin's basketball team was having a mother-son dance. Gavin really wanted to go. He wanted to go with just his mom and not have me along. I knew that this was super important to both him and Camre, but I was worried. *What if Camre had a seizure? What if she needed me and I wasn't there?* All those all fears and feelings about not having been with her when Gavin was born returned. I couldn't put the responsibility for Camre on a little boy who just wanted to have fun. Fortunately one of her best friends, who knows all about the seizures and other issues, volunteered to go along with her. That made me feel better, but I still wondered if maybe I should go to the dance and secretly hang out in the parking lot just in case.

The day before Camre and I had bought Gavin a new outfit to surprise him. We got him some brown dress boots, a pair of khakis, a collared blue shirt, and a new belt—a whole new outfit. We had laid it out on his bed when we picked him up from school. He went into the room and

92

came out bursting with excitement. "Mommy, Daddy. Thank you so much!" When he woke up the morning of the dance, he wanted to get dressed right away, but we persuaded him to wait until the afternoon. Finally, about 2:30, after he had finished target practice, we told him he could get ready.

Camre and I were sitting on the couch waiting for him to show us how he looked when Camre said, "Hey." It was our signal. When she says "hey" in that particular tone, I know that she is going into a seizure. I immediately grabbed the child-proof bottle of epilepsy medication that I keep with me at all times and put three of them under her tongue. All the while I was praying that we could stop it before it started. I swiped the VNS magnet across her chest. Unfortunately, neither the medication nor the VNS worked. She went into a grand mal seizure and a bad one at that.

Now Gavin has seen his mom have seizures before and while they upset him, in some ways he has gotten used to them. I'm always amazed at how calm he is when he sees one. One day Camre had a seizure while I was outside. He called me on my cell and said, "Daddy, Mom is having a seizure. You better come back in right away." But this seizure upset him more than usual.

"Oh no," he cried. "She's having one of them. That means we can't go to the dance." He crinkled his nose and tried not to tear up as I turned Camre's head to one side and held her in my arms.

"It's okay, buddy," I said. "Your mom's tough. She is going to make it out of this and you are going to go to the dance. Don't worry about it. It's going to be all right." You might think that I was just trying to reassure him, but I know Camre. I knew that as soon as she was out of the seizure, no matter how awful she felt, she was going to do everything she could to make it to the dance.

The seizure was a tough one. It lasted more than four minutes and, to put it mildly, it kicked her butt. Once she came out of it, she laid on the couch for about a half hour. When she was finally able to sit up, she ran to the bathroom room and began throwing up. The seizure had triggered a major migraine. She came out of the bathroom, only to run back in. She was in really bad shape. I couldn't help but think back when she wasn't able to go to her shower before Gavin was born. Now, just when she was finally going to get to experience a normal mom/son moment, this had to happen.

"Is Mommy going to be able to go the dance?" Gavin asked, his eyes wide with concern.

"I don't know," I told him sadly. "But let's just wait a little longer and see. Your mom is really strong and if she can make it, she will."

The plan had been for Camre's friend to pick Camre and Gavin up and go out to dinner before the dance. I thought maybe that if we waited long enough, Camre might be able to go to the dance for a little while even if they couldn't go out to dinner.

She came out of the bathroom. I told her what I was thinking. "No way," she said. "Gavin really wants to go out to eat, so I'm going to try to go." She immediately headed back to the bathroom and threw up again. I hated to see her like that. Most of all, I hated to see our little boy so disappointed. He took it bravely, but I could see in his eyes that he was as sad as he had ever been in his life. He had counted on this evening so much. Each time she came out of the bathroom, I began to doubt she could pull it together, but I never let on to Gavin.

In between times throwing up, Camre got dressed for the dance. She managed to stop throwing up long enough to take some pictures in our front yard. She is so strong and so good at not letting anyone see her pain, you would never know that immediately after the picture-taking was over, she threw up again. All in all, she threw up six times.

By then her friend had arrived. I explained what had happened and gave her the opportunity to back out. She wasn't having any of it. "Don't worry," her friend said. "We can handle it."

"If you need me, just give me a call. I'll be right there." I was still planning to follow them to the dance and wait in my car in the parking lot. That way I could be there in minutes.

"Steve," her friend said firmly, as if she suspected my plan. "Thank you for letting me take your family. You just sit back and relax. It will be fine."

Since the likelihood of Camre's having a second seizure that night was remote, I took a deep breath and trusted it would work out. As they walked out the door to go to the restaurant, I got down on my knees and gave Gavin a big hug. "Buddy, I hope you have the time of your life. Keep an eye on your mom for me, but just have fun with your mother and your friends."

"Thanks, Daddy," he said, wiggling with excitement to get going.

I gave Camre a kiss and reminded her that I would be right there if she needed me. "I am so proud of you!" I said. She smiled, even though I could tell that her head was still killing her. I hoped that the Advil she had taken would kick in so that she would be able to enjoy at least some of the dance. As they drove away, I started to go to my truck to drive to the parking lot, then changed my mind. This was their time. Camre's and Gavin's time. I knew they didn't need me keeping an eye on them. I also knew I couldn't just sit around waiting for them to come home, so I decided to go to a nearby golf course and hit a few balls. I love to play golf but rarely get to do it. This was my chance to do something for me as well as for them.

I'll admit I texted once during the dance, but mostly I just gave them their space.

I got home about 7:30 and expected them to arrive any minute. Much to my surprise and maybe a little concern, they didn't get home until nine. I was eating a bowl of cereal when I saw the headlights come down our drive. I raced outside.

"How was it?" I asked.

"It was great," Camre said. "I had a wonderful night. I was just like all the other moms. I talked with them. Gavin played with his friends. I had a great time. Sorry to be late," she added, "but we decided to go out for ice cream afterwards." She had no idea how delighted I was to hear that. After all that had happened, all that we had gone through, Camre was finally experiencing what she had always wanted—being a regular mom, doing normal mom things like going out for ice cream after a mother/son dance.

"What about you, buddy? Did you have a good time?"

Gavin jumped into my arms and gave me a huge hug. "Daddy, Daddy, I had the best time of my life."

I drew his mom into our embrace. Holding my wife and our son under a star-studded sky, all I could think was that no matter what happened in the future, we were a family and always would be.

We got this.

About the Authors

Steve and *Camre Curto* live in Linden, Michigan. They do as many normal things as they can, including attending Gavin's sports and school activities and going on family vacations. In addition, they continue to explore cutting-edge medical treatment for epilepsy and are hopeful that one day, Camre will be seizure-free. Camre continues regular therapy to retrain her brain, enjoys feeding the wildlife on their property, and playing with her big slobbery dog. Steve is pursuing a career in real estate, as well as being a caregiver for Camre and dad to Gavin. In his free time, he coaches Little League and basketball, and golfs once in a while.

Woodeene Koenig-Bricker lives in Eugene, Oregon. A journalist, founding editor of a parenting magazine, and speaker, she is the author of ten books and thousands of articles.

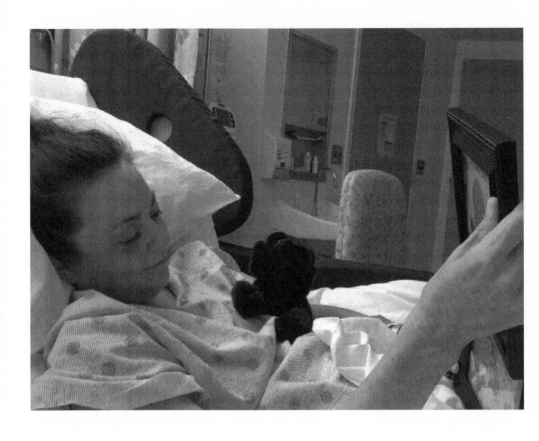

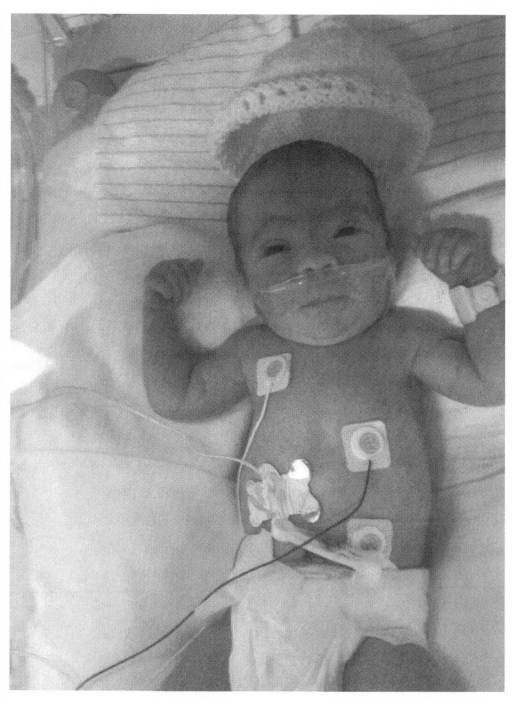

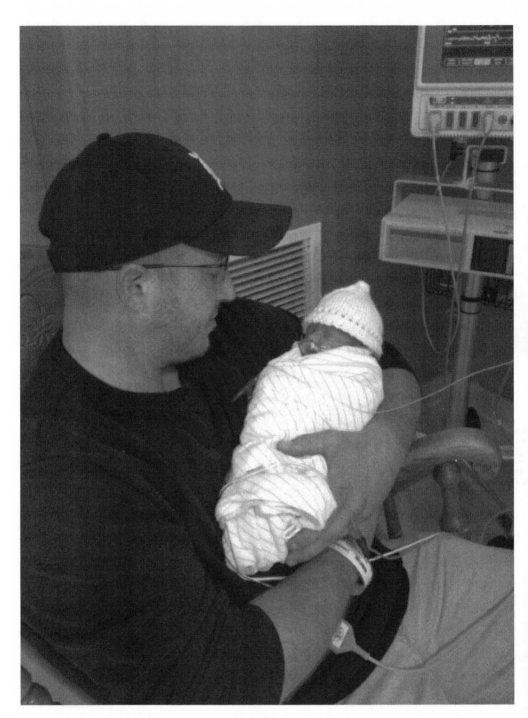